CYCLE SYNC *Your Business*

How to Leverage

Your Menstrual Cycle

for More Income and Impact

Within Your Business

Renae Fieck

ISBN PRINT: 979-8-9911973-0-4

ISBN EBOOK: 979-8-9911973-1-1

Editing by Lyric D., Sara Kazmierski, and Carly Catt

Photography by Michelle Adams

Graphic Design by Renae Fieck

www.RenaeFieck.com

To every period that has been shed without realizing its truest potential.

Contents

Introduction
Allow It to Be

Chances are if you picked up this book, you're looking for one of three things . . .

- A way to grow your business and achieve bigger goals in a way that doesn't burn you out.
- A system that allows you to do *all* the things you want to do in a way that feels balanced and aligned with who you are as a woman.
- A deeper understanding of how women were actually designed to work.

If that's you, I've got you and you're in the right place.

Generally, I find that women that I work with are making major strides in their business but it's coming at a cost.

That cost might be time with their family, skipped workouts and decreasing health, suffering mental health, failed relationships, etc. Many women are struggling to manage all the demands of raising a family and thriving business at the same time.

There are so many messages promising that it's possible to do both. Sadly, many women spend lots of time trying to make it work and then either burn out or give up on their dreams because it's so much for women to carry.

The intent behind the book is to help provide you with the answer. My intent within the pages of this book is to show you how women were designed differently and how this impacts literally every area of your life. And it's likely something you've never been taught before.

Throughout this book I'll weave together biological, spiritual, and philosophical ideas that will shift the way you view your work and show up in your life every single day. A word of caution that this book may challenge your current ways of thinking. It may go against societal expectations or belief systems you've previously held. It may also be outside of what you have heard before regarding "a feminine business." The journey of expanding beyond your current way of existence can be a little disorienting. If that occurs, just allow yourself to be with the concepts, try them on, and discern what's meant for you.

Resist the Urge to Do and Allow It to Be

As you move throughout this book, you may feel the urge to "do" and start implementing all the changes that you read about in the book, which is great. We need to take action and make shifts in order to create changes.

Oftentimes in the business world there's so much focus on doing and working. We see results and success as a byproduct of the effort we put in. Yet have you ever seen someone (maybe even yourself) working their rear off with nothing to show for it?

One of the feminine qualities I've been learning to embrace is the essence of allowing. Rather than forcing, pushing, or making something happen, can we find peace and ease in allowing it to just be?

Allowing work to be easy.

Allowing it to be fun.

Allowing it to be enjoyable.

Allowing it to be pleasurable . . . and abundant.

That urge to allow is there for a reason, and I hope you walk away from this book with the permission to start following those urges. Those small whispers of your body. The small whispers of your intuition guiding you to where you're meant to be, even when it doesn't seem logical or reasonable.

As you begin applying the concepts in this book, my hope is that you begin to trust yourself. There is so much noise in the world, and very rarely are we taught to turn inward for guidance. My desire is that this book helps you begin that inward journey back to yourself so you reconnect with yourself and learn to trust yourself again.

And allow yourself to just be.

Be all of you...the messy, raw, beautiful, crazy, silly, emotional, focused, and all other parts that make you who you truly are. When we allow ourselves to fully be ourselves and allow ourselves to embrace the season and phase, that's when true peace begins to emerge.

So let's do this!

♡ Renae

Chapter 1:
Redefining the Hustle

In college, I was a straight-A student, took more than a full load of classes, worked at Red Robin serving tables on the weekends, and worked an on-campus job during the week. How I still managed to have an active social life and go on dates with my now husband is beyond me. The hustle was real. There was always something to do. A deadline to meet. Somewhere I had to be. At the time it felt okay, but I think if I were truly honest with myself, I was going so fast I didn't actually have the time to slow down and check in with myself. I was running on a heavy dose of cortisol and adrenaline.

I was having major period issues but was away at college and didn't have a primary doctor. With a family history of thyroid issues, massively irregular periods, and some other symptoms that I can't even remember at this point, I got desperate for help. I spent less than fifteen minutes with a doctor, five minutes getting labs drawn, and thirty minutes in recovery after I passed out and took out an entire plant in the waiting room on my way out. Those lab results came back . . . *normal.* Nothing was diagnosable, my symptoms were dismissed, I was prescribed birth control as a fix and sent along on my merry way. No one even mentioned the possibility that the high stress I was putting my body under was creating a full-body response on not just my reproductive hormones but every system within my body and that this response was the cause of many of the symptoms I was experiencing.

Fast-forward eight years later when I had my first baby. The busyness of those days was replaced with an entirely new type of busyness. If you're a mom, you know exactly what I'm talking about. There were days when I felt like I accomplished *nothing* and yet I was busy from the moment I woke to the moment I went to bed. Picking up the laundry, doing the dishes, changing diapers, literally every waking moment was filled with something. Even the moments when I allowed myself to rest and snuggle with my baby, there was this feeling that I needed to "be productive." So even playing with my baby or snuggling with her, I was intentional and had a purpose . . . whether it was bonding or for her development (pediatric occupational therapist here, can't help that one!).

There was this constant compulsion to be productive all the time. And I don't think I'm alone in this feeling. Many of my clients have expressed this guilt for slowing down and stopping because there's always something that needs to be done. Heaven forbid you actually stop for a moment when there's something on the list to be done, right?

Historically, women have always juggled a lot. Even as far back as the 1700s, women were caring for their family through managing their farms, making breads to sell, weaving clothes, etc., all while raising their kids. As time progressed through the 1800s and 1900s, work moved off the farms and into factories and jobs outside the home. By 1920, women made up 20% of the workforce, and they quickly grew to 47% of the workforce by the 1950s.[1] While women made this transition into the workforce, we continued to raise our kids and tend to our homes while also having to "prove" our worthiness for things such as equal pay, job positions, and equality in the office. Women in the USA only gained the right to own a bank account in just 1974.[2] Can we just stop there for a moment and reflect on that date? 1974?! It's been less than fifty years since women have had the right to manage their own money. Prior to that, they had to have a male relative own an account for them if they wanted to place money in the bank.

Now in 2023, we have women running multimillion-dollar businesses. We've seen women achieving far more success outside of the home than ever before. We've literally kicked ass in amazing and beautiful ways. In fact, in the past twenty years we've seen a massive rise in women-owned businesses with nearly 39% of businesses today women owned and generating more than $2.7 trillion in revenue.[3] Unlike any other time in history, we have the opportunity today to create and lead businesses that support a work environment more conducive for women. Yet in the midst of most of this growth and success, women have predominantly remained the caretakers within their homes and with their kids. We're now running businesses, coaching our kids' soccer teams, cooking

---

[1] Janet L. Yellen, "The history of women's work and wages and how it has created success for us all," Brookings.edu, 2017, https://www.brookings.edu/articles/the-history-of-womens-work-and-wages-and-how-it-has-created-success-for-us-all/.

[2] Jamela Adam, "When Could Women Open A Bank Account?" *Forbes*, March 20, 2023, https://www.forbes.com/advisor/banking/when-could-women-open-a-bank-account/.

[3] "The 2024 Impact of Women-Owned Businesses" j(PDF), Wells Fargo, 2024, https://www.wippeducationinstitute.org/_files/ugd/5cba3e_96b999d23fb04d8eb488192a1 79781d4.pdf.

homemade organic meals, and keeping a decluttered house all at the same time. Just a generation or two ago, women were managing half the roles women today are carrying. There was far more space for women to just breathe.

The age of technology has forced us to move faster, perform more, and do it more perfectly, while millions of people on social media are watching us try to keep up with it. Now we're inundated daily with the pressures of cutting our kids' lunches into tiny hearts and stars, hitting six figures in ninety days, and being the Pinterest-worthy woman. It's a ton of pressure that can leave even the most organized and productive woman feeling like she's not quite enough.

It's left women juggling a million things on their plates and feeling like they can't put any of it down. When they do, they begin to feel guilty. Guilty when they focus on their business instead of their kids or guilty when they close the computer for some rest when they know they have a list of to-dos. It's a catch-22 with nearly any action leading down the road to guilt.

Women with massively big goals can be left feeling like the only way to achieve them is to muscle through and keep trying to do it all. Women feel motivated and excited and then quickly become burnt out. Or they go years running on fumes until something in their life suffers, like their health (talk about cortisol overload), relationships, sanity, or family.

Yet the true struggle is that for many of us, we have this deep longing to do it all. We want to create freedom, make an impact, and live out our biggest visions while still being true to ourselves and present for our families.

A few years ago I hired a coach whose messaging stated she used a feminine approach to grow her business to $100,000 in less than a year. After working with her, I realized that while her business was successful, she was struggling with anxiety and depression. She was struggling with body image and relationship issues. Her "feminine approach" didn't mean anything other than that she was a woman. She was still using strategies that focused on effort and hustle and pushing to your goals. Truly, she was approaching her business from a heavy, masculine approach, and it was burning her out.

This is the way I see most women building their businesses . . . relying on masculine strategies while infusing it with some pink and swirly fonts and calling it "feminine." That's not what this book is about. This book is going to empower you to understand how your body and hormones impact your body and also the power (and need) for both the masculine and feminine energies within business.

For the first three years of my business, I had attempted to build my business in that same way. It's no surprise the hustler in me decided to start my own business the year my husband was diagnosed with a brain tumor while I continued raising three kids and working two part-time jobs. Call me crazy, yes, but that dream to create more freedom in my life was strong. There was something in my soul longing to slow down and savor the moments. Still, hustling was the only thing I knew, and feeling out of balance felt like my only option.

I was willing to do anything and everything it took to make my dreams a reality. When my network marketing company recommended reaching out and connecting with three new people each day, I would reach out and talk to a hundred. I was 100% committed. *More* than 100% committed.

After a few years, I started to notice the weight of that commitment. I was getting up early and going to bed late, leaving me physically drained and exhausted. I was reaching out to any and every person I possibly could share with about my "opportunity." (I cringe thinking back to those early days of my business.) At the end of my second year, I went to file our taxes. I realized I hadn't tracked a single expense in our personal or business accounts because every ounce of free time I had was going toward building and growing a business. I'd neglected many of the basic things in our lives, like managing expenses, in pursuit of the goals I'd set. I was frustrated with the effort I'd been putting in and the lack of freedom I was feeling.

All the experts, coaches, and leaders I was following encouraged that unhealthy mentality: "Your dreams don't work unless you do" or "Find a way, not an excuse." If I was being completely honest, I 100% believed them (at the time), and they did motivate me to get started. But after three years of building my business and paying more money than I was earning, checking all the metaphorical boxes and still not seeing the success I desired, I was tired. I knew my *why* was big enough. I was making the sacrifices (in ways I now regret), yet something was still not working. I was burning out in many ways.

When I reached my rock-bottom moment and wondered if building a business and creating this vision of freedom was in fact even possible, I thought I was alone. I thought I was the only one struggling to grow my business in the way I wanted while juggling all the other demands of life. I thought I was the only one struggling with all the sacrifices I was making (ones that really mattered, but remember, that *why* was so big I was willing to do what it took). I thought I was the only one struggling with a short temper and minimal patience with my family because I was feeling so stretched thin.

A few years after hiring the coach I referenced earlier, I started to see other big leaders in the online industry talking about the sacrifices they had made to build their businesses. There were some who even publicly declared that it wasn't worth it. One day I read a post that said something along the lines of "I hustled to grow my business throughout my twenties. I hit massive goals and focused solely on achieving them. Now I'm in my thirties and I look back and feel like I wasted my twenties. I didn't actually live them and enjoy those years because I was focused only on my business's success." Ouch.

And she's not the only one.

In recent months I've seen a swing in industry leaders reclaiming themselves. Women sharing about their journeys to reclaim their health, relationships, time, hobbies, and mental health. They're now allowing themselves to rest, work out at the gym, go on date nights, close the computer, go to therapy. While I'm super happy and excited for them to be on this journey to reclaiming themselves now, I think as women we can do better. We can learn from their journeys to pave a different way of doing business.

The business industry is plagued with messages around achieving your goals with quick fixes. There are constant messages about how to achieve our goals faster and easier. And while I'm all for being more efficient and hitting my goals faster, sacrificing things you value shouldn't be required to do it. My social media feed is riddled with posts claiming $0–100K in 90 days or $10K months in 30 days. People are craving speed and instant gratification. Yet how much is this speed costing us?

That's a big question. Even as I reread this chapter during the editing phase, I have to pause and think about the gravity of this question on a larger scale. So, before you just read past and move on, take a second and think about that question. Take a few extra minutes to ponder . . . how much is the desire for speed costing us?

There's a Better Way to Do Business

I 100% believe there is a better way of doing business. There is a way to build our businesses that focuses on what it truly takes to reach the end goal. There is a way to integrate the masculine (achieving the goals) and the feminine (enjoying the journey and process) within our businesses. It might take longer (or maybe it won't!), but wouldn't it be more worthwhile to achieve your goals and still enjoy coaching your kids' soccer games, going on date nights with your spouse, traveling, working out, and taking care of your health along the way? If you are feeling lit up on life, you're more likely to perform better in business (and every other area of life), and you'll hit your goals sooner. In fact, I believe this is really truly the secret sauce to success.

Imagine how different you'd show up for your business if you sat down to work and your body felt full of energy, focused, and excited because you'd prioritized working *with* your body versus showing up tired and exhausted because you've spent every free moment pushing to achieve your goals.

It's essential that we create a balance between building our businesses and living our lives. The problem is that many women believe that balance means everything is equal, and because of that, you may find many posts on social media with women claiming that balance doesn't exist and people who strive for it are searching for a nonexistent reality. This is partially true.

The definition of balance is a "condition in which different elements are equal or in the correct proportions," but that doesn't mean everything has to be equal *all the time*. All parts of our lives getting equal attention all the time is a fallacy. It's a standard we're likely to never achieve. And if we ever did, we probably wouldn't enjoy balancing it all the time anyway.

So what if we redefined balance to better fit our needs and desires? What if instead of striving for perfect balance between all parts of our lives, we instead looked to create a rhythm and a flow that feels good in our bodies? What if we focused on working *with* ourselves versus against it?

That may seem far-fetched right now, but I promise there is a way, and it has to do with a vital part of our being that we live with every day: our menstrual cycle!

Many amazing and wonderful things don't come quickly. They take time to cultivate, grow, and bloom. When we rush the process, it changes the outcomes.

I am so grateful for my mentor and friend, Sarah Try, for introducing me to the idea of cycle syncing and how respecting and honoring your menstrual cycle could bring ease into your world. It seems like now would be the time I say, "and the rest was history," and in some ways it was, but as a breastfeeding postpartum mom who still hadn't started cycling again, I wasn't really sure. It almost felt a little too woo-woo for me, an occupational therapist whose practice is deeply rooted in biology and science. So I started slow. I noticed there was one week of the month I could "feel" way more than others, and so I started leaning into a rhythm based around that week (more to come on this in coming chapters).

I didn't change anything. I just started to *notice* how I was feeling and recognize patterns. Over the next year or two, I started shifting small things, like being more intentional about when I sat down to write emails or when I would push harder in my business, and I noticed how much easier things felt. I started noticing times of the day when I worked better than others. Times of the month when I felt like I could get in the flow easier or when I felt more motivated or when I wanted to burn down my business.

For years I was "noticing" and making small tweaks and changes until I started sharing my progress in my membership for moms. The mind-blown emojis that followed and the messages saying "This just makes so much sense" and "Why weren't we taught this before" is what has brought me to where I am today. If it were possible for women like you and me to feel permission to lay down the hustle and rest without feeling guilty or to create the space for our next million-dollar ideas ('cause legitimately they can't come in if we're always busy) or if it were possible for women to create thriving businesses while still being present with their families, why would I keep it to myself?

Now you get to be one of those women I share it with next . . . and I can't wait!

Your Menstrual Cycle Is the Missing Link to Creating Balance

More than just aligning to our hormones, syncing with our cycle and creating this rhythm and flow in our lives allows us to actually feel whole as humans because it allows us to fulfill our four core needs of rest, creation, connection, and self-awareness. The hormones of each phase of your cycle shift throughout the month, changing the way you feel. When you honor each one of these phases and allow your life to adjust with them, it creates a rhythm to meet each of these needs. This is one of the core reasons I believe that cycling is meant for all women regardless of menstruation status. We were designed to operate within nature's cyclical rhythm (more on this in an upcoming chapter!).

When any one of these areas is missing or lacking attention, women eventually feel out of balance, overwhelmed, or burnt out. All four of these areas are vital for feeling fulfilled. Many of the women I have worked with and taught about leveraging their cycle over the last few years have instantly noticed feeling more balanced and aligned. It's one of the first and most empowering results my clients tell me they are so grateful for after working together.

Within the pages of this book, I will show you how to use each of the menstrual cycle phases to create balance in your schedule, optimize your performance, and increase your income and impact. You'll discover how to embrace your body and feminine power to become more magnetic and begin trusting yourself and your intuition. It will have massive ripple effects not just in your business but in every part of your life.

Our Bodies Aren't Machines

Our bodies aren't machines. They can't keep going endlessly without consequences. Instead, our bodies are the vehicles that allow us to live our dream lives and pursue our wildest goals. When we honor our bodies, we begin to create more balance and achieve more without having to work so hard.

Now I'm going to warn you: cycle syncing your life and work and embracing this new rhythm and way of working doesn't always happen instantly, nor is it always "easy" (at least not in the beginning).

Side note: When I talk about "working," you might be thinking only about your actual work—whether it's a job, your side hustle, or a full-time business. I want to put a caveat on the word *work*. As an occupational therapist, I recognize there are many types of work in our lives. So, for the sake of this book, let's broaden the perspective of work to anything you "work on" in your life. It might be the laundry or dishes or launching a million-dollar project. All of it encompasses your "work."

In fact, if you're like me you've had *years* of conditioning to work hard and focus on being productive. You've likely tried for years to build habits and routines focusing on being consistent (we're going to shatter the need to be consistent each day in the next few chapters). Unlearning the years of this way of being and doing doesn't happen overnight. It's a practice. So take it one step at a time. Test something out for a while and see how you like it. And for heaven's sake . . . give yourself the permission to shift and adjust and find what feels aligned for you. You can breathe a sigh of relief knowing you don't have to make any major changes or uproot your entire calendar to start tapping into this new paradigm and a new way of working all at once.

We are *all* incredibly unique and what works for me may not be the gold-star method for you. It's time that we stop looking to everyone else for the answers and instead start tuning in and asking ourselves, "What do I need right now?"

Are You Ready?

If you're like me and many of the clients I've worked with, you might not even know *how* to actually enjoy play or rest anymore. Don't worry. I've got you.

If you are the woman who does the work day in and day out but you're tired from doing it all and want a way to work without it feeling like so much . . . I've got you, boo!

If you have a big dream and vision in your heart that you *know* you're meant to bring to the world but you just aren't sure you have the capacity to add it into all your demands, you're in the right place.

Ready to unlock your biggest, greatest, and most creative (those million-dollar) ideas that feel aligned and meant for you?

Heck yes, you are! That's why you're here.

"I thought something was wrong with me. My business and life would fluctuate and I'd get so overwhelmed. Now when I'm in my head and negative…I take a deep breath and know it's just the phase of my cycle. I know if I can do what I need to support my body, I'll get through it so much easier. I get so much more done now than I ever did before. I feel so much better about myself."

—*Sara B., Your Cycle Advantage Client*

A Word of Caution

Now before you go kicking off your shoes and expect your business to be all smooth sailing by using your menstrual cycle and feminine rhythms, let's set something straight. Growth both personally and professionally isn't always comfortable. Sometimes it is challenging and pushes us to the edges of our limits. When we build muscle that's literally what we do: tear muscle fibers so they grow thicker when they rebuild.

Don't expect to read this book and think you can sit back and watch your dreams take off without putting any sweat into it.

You will have to work. You will have to do the dang thing. The difference is when you do the work in sync with your cycle, it feels less like work. When you're in alignment with what you're doing and how you're doing it and then *when* you're doing it, it just feels simpler. There might still be a few late nights and early mornings when you're in the middle of a launch. There may still be times you skip the coffee dates to get your project done. You might still have to tell the kids they have to wait a moment till you can finish the dishes. The difference is that we don't keep going on that hustle train forever. Those moments of push are for just a season or a phase.

So if you're one of those people who shies away from doing the work (the inner work or the physical work), this book may not be the answer for you.

Here's one last caution before we get into the real juicy stuff. There may be things I say that ruffle a few of your feathers. Some of it may even have you downright angry with me. (Trust me, it happens!) Going back to my word of the book . . . *allow* that to be okay. We've had centuries of conditioning into our current structures and ways of being. We've had generations of shame, trauma, and secrecy around our cycles. Menstrual huts were used around the world to ostracize women who were on their periods even as recently as 2005 due to beliefs around periods bringing bad luck, health, or being dirty.[4] Women and girls were left in these huts

---

[4] Geeta Pandey, "Banished for bleeding: Tribal Indian women get better period huts," BBC, June 3, 2021, https://www.bbc.com/news/world-asia-india-57335518.

with limited supplies and support. Through many eras and societies, taboos and stigmas existed and continue to exist today.

In many circles and environments, talking about your period is unacceptable. One study indicated that 50% of men surveyed believe it's inappropriate to talk about periods within the workplace (even though it impacts the way women function every single day).[5] In order for women to be successful in a male-driven society where acknowledging our periods is so taboo, we've had to fit in and conform to the systems and structures that are conducive and supportive for the way men work.

As you read this book and begin to embrace your cycle, hormones, and femininity in the way you work, you're literally helping to redefine the way women work and turning a whole system upside down. There may be things that just click and have you wondering, "Why didn't I know this before? This just makes so much sense." And then others that you have to sit with or leave you feeling disoriented and questioning whether it is working or not. The disorientation phase can be normal. You may receive push-back from spouses, partners, friends, or others in your circles. Find yourself a circle of women who are on this journey too. I have a client-only Facebook community called the Cycle Circle.

---

[5] Lizzie Thomson, "A third of men think it's unprofessional to talk about periods at work." Metro.uk, November 15, 2019, https://metro.co.uk/2019/11/15/a-third-of-men-think-its-unprofessional-to-talk-about-periods-at-work-11149780/.

https://renaefieck.com/bookbonuses

You're welcome to join our community. Just request to join and let us know you have this book.

Have you ever seen one of those kids' puzzles that have two different pictures, one on each side? Once you have the whole picture put together on one side, you have to turn the puzzle upside down and start again to see the new picture on the opposite side. As we navigate through these pages, I may turn the metaphorical puzzle of your life and the way you view your business and time upside down. Give yourself the space to put the puzzle back together again. I guarantee when you do, you'll find the picture even more stunning than it is now.

If you're still with me and you're ready to redefine the way you work, I seriously can't wait to watch what unfolds for you.

Chapter 2:
Why the 24-Hour Work Schedule Isn't Designed for Women

When my kids were younger and I was a stay-at-home mom, the days were bloody exhausting. There were days I didn't want to even hear the name "Mom" called one more time because it felt like I was constantly needed at all times. My body often felt touched out. It felt like my days were spent constantly putting out fires of mess. Even the "fun" projects and activities with my kids turned into a glittery paint mess that I then had the joy of cleaning. It felt like a hamster wheel of the same things over and over again each day: making meals, fighting with the kids to take a nap, doing laundry, repeat. I'd start counting down the hours till my husband would get home from work. If he wasn't home by 5:30 p.m., he would get a text from me saying, "Where the heck are you?" with me hoping to offload the kids onto him for a micro break. But he'd come home from work exhausted from the day too. Within the first hour or two of being home, I'd find him sitting on the toilet taking for-freaking-ever. In those moments I could feel the frustration brewing, and it would often end in some heated conversations.

Then one day I was chatting with a girlfriend and she said that her husband would get home from work and sit in the car in the driveway (or even down the road just a ways so the kids wouldn't see him) for thirty minutes before coming in the house. After a long day with the kids, she felt frustrated that he was getting some quiet alone time in the car. Then I started talking with friends who all said their husbands did the same thing and it often was a source of contention and frustration in their relationships. Chances are if you live with a man, you've noticed a similar pattern. It was a pattern that I began hearing from many women about their male partners. Maybe he sits on the toilet forever or takes a break for happy hour with friends after work or sits in the driveway before coming in to face the rest of the evening with the family. I'm about to shed so much light on why, and while those habits may have been infuriating before (they certainly were for me), you might find a little more grace and acceptance of them now.

Men have testosterone that generally starts at its highest earliest in the morning and then follows their natural circadian rhythm throughout the day, leaving them with less at the end of the day. They go to bed and then wake the next morning with a fresh dose of testosterone (of course, there's always some variability).[6]

---

[6] Donald J. Brambilla, Alvin M. Matsumoto, Andre B. Araujo, and John B. McKinlay, "The Effect of Diurnal Variation on Clinical Measurement of Serum Testosterone and Other Sex Hormone Levels in Men," *J Clin Endocrinol Metab.* *94*, no. 3 (2009): 907–913, https://doi.org/10.1210%2Fjc.2008-1902.

Here's a typical **hormone cycle for men.**

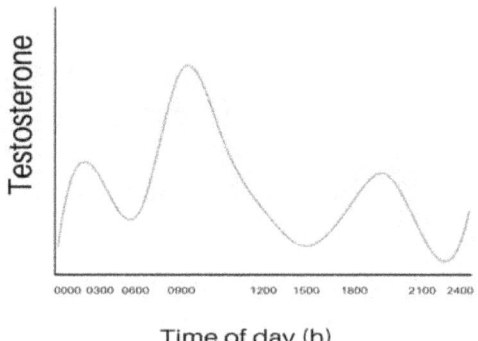

Time of day (h)

This is why men function so well on a daily rhythm with scheduling in blocks of time for working, habit-stacking their workouts at specific times of day, and waking and sleeping at the same time. The daily habits and routines thrive with this consistent rhythm. It's also why a lot of men come home from a long day at work and just need a moment of downtime (whether that's on the toilet, in their car, or on the couch). Their energy is depleted from the day, and in order to face the chaos of life in the evenings (please tell me it's not just my days with three kids that are chaos), they need a little recharge in that late afternoon.

Rather than testosterone functioning in a daily rhythm, women have predominantly estrogen and progesterone that are doing a dynamic dance throughout the entire month.

Now let's take a look at **women's hormonal cycle.**

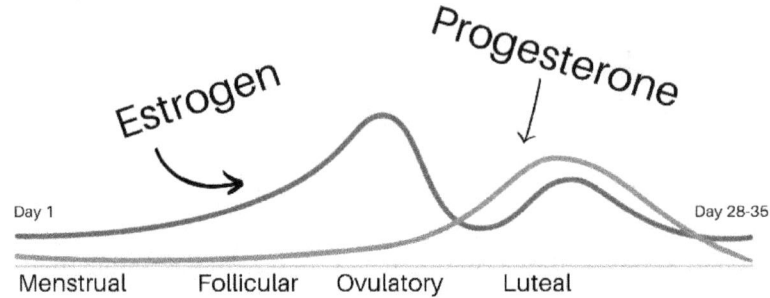

If you look at the entire month cycle, there is literally not a single day that is exactly the same as another when it comes to your hormones. So while men might be getting these microdoses of recharging every day, you might feel like one week you're high on energy and super productive and another week you just can't seem to muster any energy to get it together. The feelings are real. Estrogen and progesterone feel very different in your body and our bodies have very different needs depending on whether we're in an estrogen-dominant phase or a progesterone-dominant phase. Women weren't designed to have a consistent nutrition plan, exercise plan, or work schedule the entire month long. As we go into the next few chapters, we'll dive into exactly what each of those weeks throughout the month feel like and how to actually use them so that we don't feel like we have only one or two "good" weeks of the month while the other weeks feel railroaded by low energy or motivation.

But for now . . . did you just breathe a sigh of relief knowing that trying to be consistent every day wasn't really designed for women? Or that it's completely normal to be motivated and excited about a new workout routine or project one week and then to be dragging and forcing yourself a week or two later? When I share this inside my workshops, the light bulbs go off and so many women begin to realize the way they've felt for so long wasn't them going crazy but was actually based in our biology.

We've been taught to see time as linear and that it's all equal. If you opened a blank calendar, it would all look the same. You could pop in an appointment at any point throughout the week. It wouldn't matter where you put it. Yet have you ever said yes to something and then a week or two later you were dreading having to do it? Or maybe you've noticed that Monday doesn't feel the same as Friday? Or summer doesn't feel the same as winter? Chances are you're like me and you just gave a resounding, "Heck no! They don't feel the same," which is why when we look at our calendars and our schedules, it just makes sense to schedule things based around where you're going to be the most optimized to do that task, right?

Your hormones play a key factor in when and how you should schedule your life. They literally impact *everything*. They impact the way you think, how creative you are, how well you focus, how much seggsy time you want, and how easy it is for you to lose your mind on your kids. Who you are and how you feel on day seven of your cycle is completely different from how you feel on day twenty-one and throughout the entire month.

Recently I came across a research study that used MRIs throughout the menstrual cycle to show the physiological changes that happen to the brain with the changes in estrogen and progesterone.[7] Throughout the month, the activated parts of your brain completely change. For example, some days of the month your emotional centers of your brain are on fire, while other times of the month your logical, critical reasoning centers have more flow. And your brain is just one area of your body that's impacted by the hormone shifts of your menstrual cycle.

Estrogen and progesterone impact nearly every system in your body. Estrogen is the hormone we can thank for our rising libido (sex drive), elevated mood, and muscle building. It also stabilizes our blood pressure, lowers cholesterol, and supports our bone growth.[8] Progesterone is a key player in supporting the development of your uterine environment, your ovaries and egg development, and pregnancy by creating a healthy womb space for growing a baby.[9] It's been known to metabolize in the brain and create a calming, anti-anxiety effect as well.

Your skin vibrancy and glow changes throughout the month.[10] How you build muscle or lose fat is impacted based on

---

[7] Timothy J. Meeker, Dieuwke S. Veldhuijzen, Michael L. Keaser, Rao P. Gullapalli, and Joel D. Greenspan, "Menstrual Cycle Variations in Gray Matter Volume, White Matter Volume and Functional Connectivity: Critical Impact on Parietal Lobe," *Frontiers in Neuroscience* 14 (December 2020): 594588, https://www.ncbi.nlm.nih.gov/pmc/articles/PMC7783210; C. L. Janus, H. P. Wiczyk, and N. Laufer, "Magnetic resonance imaging of the menstrual cycle," *Magn Reson Imaging* 7, no. 6 (November 1988): 693–4, https://doi.org/10.1016/0730-725x(88)90091-4.
[8] "Estrogen: Hormone, Function, Levels & Imbalances," Cleveland Clinic, reviewed February 8, 2022, https://my.clevelandclinic.org/health/body/22353-estrogen.
[9] "Progesterone: Natural Function, Levels & Side Effects," Cleveland Clinic, December 29, 2022. https://my.clevelandclinic.org/health/body/24562-progesterone.
[10] Bethany Burgoyne, "The relationship between skin health and sex hormones," .inne, accessed August 12, 2024, https://www.inne.io/en/blog/article/the-relationship-between-skin-health-and-sex-hormones.

your hormones.[11] The salt crystals in your saliva change, and even some research points to the color and shape of your tongue changing (fascinating!).[12]

If you aren't sure you believe me yet, start tracking it. And when I say tracking "it," I'm not talking about your period; I'm talking about your entire cycle because your period is just the encore of the entire production that's happened all month long. In fact, ovulation is the key player within our cycles, and yet most women don't even know if or when they are ovulating.

Cycle Syncing Doubts

While I will acknowledge there is conflicting research regarding cycle syncing—you might even be doubting what I've shared so far—my invitation for you is to try it on. One thing I've learned in medicine and science is not everything has been adequately researched and studied. We're constantly learning new information, changing the way we practice, and adding more to areas that were once unknown. Before something is well researched and supported, there is often anecdotal research (personal stories) that precedes the scientific data research. While you may find some conflicting research in regard to cycle syncing, you will find plenty of research that demonstrates the impacts of the menstrual cycle on

---

[11] Nuria Romero-Parra, Rocio Cuperio, Victor M. Alfaro-Magallanes, Beatriz Rael, Jacobo A. Rubio-Arias, Ana B. Peinado, and Pedro J. Benito, "Exercise-Induced Muscle Damage During the Menstrual Cycle: A Systematic Review and Meta-Analysis," *Journal of Strength and Conditioning Research 35*, no. 2 (February) 2021: 549–561, https://doi.org/10.1519/JSC.0000000000003878.

[12] M. Guida, M. Barbato, P. Bruno, G. Lauro, and C. Lampariello, "Salivary ferning and the menstrual cycle in women," *Clin Exp Obstet Gynecol 20*, no. 1 (1993): 48–54, PMID: 8462188.

women when it comes to sleep, brain function, nutrition, and so much more. So wouldn't it just make sense that leaning into this rhythm would in fact help us function more optimally within our work?

When I first started tracking my cycle, I went into it with heavy doubts. It felt a bit too woo-woo and spiritual to me. I was postpartum and didn't have a cycle. Heck, between being pregnant and breastfeeding for the tenish years prior, I actually quite enjoyed not having a cycle for so many years. But curiosity kept me digging in. At the time, I could 1000% feel the luteal phase weeks. I was a raging bitch and would send my family running for cover most days that week. Those were the weeks that made me feel like I was failing at everything. There was one moment we were all in Hawaii on our ten-year anniversary trip and I got so angry that I walked away from my family and imagined never going home. I was walking down the road, calling my best friend, crying about how I couldn't do it anymore. I'm telling you, those feelings were strong and heavy (and likely postpartum, which comes with its own special hormones). At the time I didn't know about how my hormones were impacting my life, but now looking back, I'm confident that week I was in my luteal phase. If I'd known then, I would have likely given myself a whole lot more grace and space to actually feel my feelings and employed strategies to help me regulate instead of creating such a painful core memory.

How I Started Tracking

When I started tracking, I honed in on that luteal week when I felt those intense feelings and planned the rest of my month around it. Within the first two months, my period was back and more regular than it had ever been in my life. So I kept digging, learning, and researching. At first, I didn't do much with it. I just became aware of what was happening. Even just the awareness made such a shift for me. The weeks when I'd lost my shit, I'd acknowledge what was happening hormonally, and even that simple acknowledgment seemed to lighten the load.

Over time I started integrating it more and more. I became an experimenter, researching deeper, and creating my own theories and philosophies around how to support women in using their cycle and embodying a whole new way of working. I tested it within my own schedule and business for two years before I started sharing it with my clients. Once I started sharing it with other women, I was able to support them in integrating it within their own life and business. Some of them were able to double their business revenue. Some of them started taking more time off, while others finally allowed themselves to rest guilt-free. Some of them healed years of PMDD or PMS symptoms. Yet all of them couldn't believe that they were thirty to forty years old before they learned the impact of their cycle on the way they worked and showed up every day.

Whether you've been an avid tracker, you have a general awareness of your body, or you haven't paid attention at all, the key is to just start where you are. Start tracking your key metrics (period and ovulation), and then start layering in more as you learn more. All the information you gain from tracking and beginning to listen to your body won't just benefit your work; it will have impacts and ripples into many areas of your life. If you want access to the tracker I use and give my clients, you can grab it on the resources page.

https://renaefieck.com/bookbonuses

A Note On Masculinity and Femininity

Men and women are different both biologically and physiologically. And that is okay! It's actually really beautiful.

There are some books and experts I've read that lead with the "down with patriarchy" or "toxic masculinity" ideas and cast a negative lens on the masculine parts of us. That's not my intent with this book. There is masculinity within us (and our society), and we need that. The world needs it. Don't get me wrong . . . there may be changes that need to happen in our society and the patriarchy, but we don't have to throw out the baby with the bath water. The problem is that when women are living their lives in accordance with the twenty-four-hour calendar versus the twenty-eight-day calendar, there is often more of an emphasis on masculinity. The focus becomes on being consistent each day, being productive, and getting more done. But I truly don't believe it's an either-or.

We need both the masculine and the feminine energies to coexist within our world. The masculine energy helps us do and create big actions. It's logical, clear, and helps us focus on where we're going. It helps us create structures and systems so we operate more efficiently. The feminine energy, on the other hand, helps us find flow and move in tune with our intuition. It helps us empathize, connect, feel, and create from within. The feminine within us can defy logic and reasoning and resides within this "gut" knowing. Predominantly, masculine energy resides in the head space, while feminine energy resides more within the heart and womb.

Even within our own cycles, we have both elements of the masculine and the feminine. We all have elements of feminine and masculine, despite whatever gender we identify as. It's not about creating equality between masculinity and femininity or one dominating over the other, but instead allowing for the coexistence of both. It's in the coexistence and the duality of holding both of these opposing energies at the same time that helps us to create the perfect harmony. You can embrace your femininity and your masculinity. You can pursue big goals and ambitions while being in flow with your cycle and intuition.

You can do this by learning to trust yourself. Trust your intuition. Trust your body. Chances are you haven't had many messages teaching you to listen in and trust your own body when it comes to how you live, much less how you work. There's always someone with advice on how you should live, eat, sleep, etc. Literally as I opened social media today, within the first five minutes, I was faced with someone telling me what I needed to eat to lose weight and the trending social posts to grow my business. Yet very rarely do you hear people saying, "What do you need? What feels right for you?" Can we really assume that every strategy, diet, or hack is going to work for every woman?

I can guarantee you that you and I are drastically different. How we build our businesses, how we spend our time, what recharges us . . . it's all going to be different. What works for me may not always work for you. And that is why I find our cycle and the twenty-eight-day calendar so magical. It brings us back to listening to our bodies. It brings us back to ourselves. And that, my friend, is where the magic lies.

While this book was written with a focus on women who identify as women and were born as anatomical women, it is important to recognize that gender identity and expression are diverse and unique to each individual. The terms "femininity" and "masculinity" used throughout this book do not strictly refer to female or male bodies but rather to the different energies that exist within all of us, regardless of our gender identity. These energies are universal and can be embraced by anyone, regardless of how they identify. Whether you resonate with the feminine, the masculine, or any combination of energies, you are welcome here. While this book often uses the words "female" and "male" or "woman" it is not intended to exclude those who identify otherwise. This book aims to support everyone in understanding and harnessing these powerful forces to create balance and harmony in business and life.

If you read through this book and don't feel inspired to work differently, or if you try syncing your work and life to your cycle and it doesn't make a difference for you, that's a-okay! Embodying your feminine within is ultimately about learning to trust your inner guidance and find that thing that works for you. Whether that inner guidance is your cycle, your intuition, your body, or something else entirely, learning to trust yourself is the core of what I want you to walk away with. **When you trust yourself** rather than searching for the answers in everyone else or what you've been told, your life will truly begin to change.

Chapter 3:
What If I Don't Have a Period?

Now before we dive into the juicy stuff, I want to address this question right out of the gate . . . "What if I don't have a period?" There are a variety of reasons why women may not have a period—pregnancy, birth control, perimenopause, menopause, hysterectomy, etc. And the question of "Will this work for me?" comes up all the time with my clients.

The first time I heard about cycle syncing I was postpartum and didn't have a period either. I timidly raised my hand in the Zoom training as she spoke about the power of our cycles and asked if it was possible to work for me too. I sort of assumed, and maybe you're assuming too, that syncing with your cycle wouldn't be possible if you didn't have a period at all.

But what I slowly started to learn is that even though I wasn't bleeding, I still had a cycle. I noticed I still had weeks when I was a raging crazy woman who made my family run for the hills. There were other weeks when I felt grounded and confident in what I was doing. There were still hormones and rhythms happening in the background. I just didn't have a period as an external guide or cue.

It was the beginning of me starting to listen to my body and sync my life to what I was feeling. I started using the four phases of my cycle to predict where I should be and began making micro adjustments to my schedule. Within just a few months, my cycle returned and became more regular than it had ever been prior. And this girl had some wildly irregular cycles before—we're talking variations of cycles of sixty days to fifteen days. It's been roughly seven years since and aside from cycle changes post-COVID, it's continued to vary between thirty and thirty-five days ever since.

Chances are if you're in that boat you may have wondered if it's possible to cycle sync with your_situation. And the answer is yes! It will just look a little different. In fact, not having a period can actually be a really good thing because at the core, syncing with your body requires you to learn and listen to the language of your body. Without a period, you must begin learning and understanding that language in a much deeper way. It can actually be the thing that gives you an advantage when it comes to leveraging your body.

The rest of this chapter will address each specific reason why you might not have a period. You can skip to the section that applies to you or read them all and understand the beauty of the female body even more. (If I were you, I'd read them all 'cause there's valuable nuggets of info in each section that will apply to all of us.)

Irregular Cycles

A few years ago, I decided I wanted to start waking up earlier in the morning. I work so much better early in the morning than I do in the evening, and I wanted a few extra hours before the kids woke up (and it's incredibly powerful when you start the day feeling like you've already been productive!). But I love my sleep. Truly. When the research all points to seven or eight hours of sleep for the average person, you can be sure I'm in the eight-to-ten-hour category. As someone who naturally got up around 7 a.m., shifting to 5:30 to 6 a.m. threw off my whole circadian rhythm.

The first few mornings I set my alarm, I'd reach over and fumble for the alarm to shut it off. I'd snooze it for at least an hour before I got up. Every morning, that alarm would go off. For the first few weeks, I rarely actually got up when the alarm went off. Then something magical began to happen; it started to become easy to get up when my alarm went off. A few more weeks and all of a sudden I was waking *before* the alarm went off. In just a few weeks—err, months—I was able to reset my circadian rhythm and allow my body to operate on a new rhythm with sleep.

When we look at your cycle, your body functions in the same way. As human beings, many of our biological systems function best with rhythms. We have many internal rhythms such as the circadian rhythm (our twenty-four-hour physiological rhythms such as sleeping), diurnal rhythms (our daily rhythm of night versus day), and infradian rhythms (our most common being the menstrual cycle). These rhythms help your body create a homeostasis and reduce the stress response. When we operate out of rhythm, our bodies experience micro-stressors. Your body and your habits have a symbiotic relationship. Your hormones impact the way you feel and how you show up. Your habits impact how your hormones operate.

If your cycles are irregular and there isn't a medical reason to blame, take a look at your habits. For many women, prior to reading this book you might have been leaning into more male-driven habits and rhythms, which ultimately can lead to sub-clinical micro-stressors. Are your habits conducive to supporting your hormones and a regular menstrual cycle? For me and many of my clients, simply starting to align our lives to our cycles has helped regulate and normalize them. It's like a reset for your body's hormone system. When our habits support a regular menstrual cycle, it's easier for our body and our hormones to function in a way that supports that regular function.

If you notice one of your phases is stronger than another and you can pinpoint which phase you might be in, start there. Then take the other three phases and overlay them over your calendar and help your body start to learn that rhythm. Use your habits to support your hormones, and over time your hormones can then support your lifestyle habits.

Our world operates on a much different schedule than it once did. Prior to the age of technology, we followed the rhythms of the earth. Humans used to change their lifestyle and patterns with the seasons of the year and the setting and rising of the moon. Today we have electricity, artificial light, and technology that allows us to create our own schedules. We can stay up late at night scrolling on social media. We can rise and get to work before the sun has risen. We can grow foods out of season and use hormones to make cows continue to produce milk. It's allowed us to produce all the time, yet that production has come at a cost. It's no wonder that our cycles and health are in disarray. We're living out of sync with the way nature was designed.

I once read that the menstrual cycles of women who lived before artificial light all synced up with the rhythm of the moon. While these are hypotheses, there is research now demonstrating that artificial lighting (phones, lights, computer screens, TVs) is impacting the regularity of your menstrual cycle and our hormone health.[13]

There are so many other things that can contribute to irregular cycles that you want to be aware of. Here are some questions to help you get started:

- *Am I getting enough sleep?*
- *Am I playing on my phone late at night and first thing in the morning?*
- *Am I eating foods that are nutrient-dense and supporting my body? Am I eating enough food?*
- *Am I constantly stressed? Could cortisol be shutting down my reproductive hormones?*
- *Do I have artificial fragrances in my house or products?*
- *Are there other chemicals or BPAs in my environment?*

---

[13] O. Hecmarie Melendez-Fernandez, Jennifer A. Liu, and Randy J. Nelson, "Circadian Rhythms Disrupted by Light at Night and Mistimed Food Intake Alter Hormonal Rhythms and Metabolism," *Int J Mol Sci.* 24, no. 4 (February 2023): 3392, https://doi.org/10.3390/ijms24043392; Konstantin V. Danilenko and Elena A. Samoilova, "Stimulatory Effect of Morning Bright Light on Reproductive Hormones and Ovulation: Results of a Controlled Crossover Trial," *PLoS Clin Trials 2*, no. 2 (February 2007): e7, https://doi.org/10.1371/journal.pctr.0020007.

There are so many small shifts we can make in our lifestyle to support us and help us return to the natural rhythm of our cycles if a medical condition isn't to blame.

If your cycle is too inconsistent to even try to sync with at this point, you can try following the cycle of the moon (see the upcoming section on syncing with the moon). Syncing with the moon helps support that natural monthly rhythm that your body was designed to operate with. I've had some clients begin syncing with the moon when their menstrual cycles were too unpredictable and noticed that within just a few months their cycles became more consistent, predictable, and regular.

Oftentimes I find that women view irregular cycles as a negative thing when it comes to cycle syncing. While having irregular cycles isn't always the healthiest thing and can be a huge indicator into what's going on inside your body hormonally, it can actually be a really good thing when we start out trying to sync with it. You see, when you don't have a regular cycle, it can be a bit more challenging to know where in the cycle you are and so this requires you to listen to your body even deeper. You begin to learn your body's cues and the language of your body in a much more intimate way. Someone who has a regular cycle could plug her period onto the calendar and rely only on the visual of the calendar. It doesn't require her to listen in to how her body truly is speaking. So if you have an irregular cycle, embrace its gift for you to learn even more about yourself and trust that over time, listening to it and trusting it, your menstrual cycle will become more rhythmic. I see many women who join my program, Your Cycle Advantage, begin to notice their cycles becoming more rhythmic even within the first few months.

Regardless of why your cycle is irregular or what tools you employ to support its regular rhythm, learning to listen to your body each day can become one of your greatest assets in so many ways.

Perimenopause/Menopause

Talk about hormone shifts. That predictable pattern you may have had years ago sort of goes out the window during perimenopause and then completely disappears in menopause. When you have a period one month and then it disappears for six months and then randomly shows up again, it can feel challenging to use and leverage your cycle in your work.

As you move into menopause, your estrogen, which once made you feel high and amazing during the follicular phase, varies and eventually plummets. While estrogen is often the hormone that contributes to most of the menopause symptoms, progesterone decreases during this phase of life as well. The normal hormone shifts of the menstrual cycle disappear and make living in this cyclical rhythm very different. Many people will even claim that cycle syncing isn't possible for women in this stage.

But I disagree.

In this phase it certainly isn't going to look like aligning with a menstrual cycle or your hormones. However, women are cyclical. Our world is cyclical. When we lean into a rhythm that supports our cycle, we create balance.

This is one of the most valuable concepts in all the work I do. The balance we can create when we get off the "produce all the time" hamster wheel is one of the most life-changing elements.

For women in perimenopause or menopause, using the moon as your external guide and rhythm can help support this cyclical rhythm and balance. It may not be something that you feel the benefits of right away, but as you support your body with this rhythm, it will continue to strengthen over time. (See the upcoming section on how to sync with the moon.) While initially your body may not understand the rhythm and you may not notice any major benefits, as you support your body with a consistent rhythm, it will learn to operate within that rhythm. (If you didn't read the section on irregular cycles, go back and read that section on the interaction of our habits and rhythms.)

If you're about to enter menopause/perimenopause, I have a special challenge for you. Based on the fact that women are cyclical and have spent a majority of their lives operating with their menstrual cycle, the transition to menopause can cause a major disruption. I have a theory that women who sync up with the moon and continue to create lifestyle habits that support a monthly rhythm will navigate through perimenopause and menopause with more ease. There's no research on this yet, and I've had other experts disagree with me. I sometimes wonder that if we start challenging the menopause journey and what's considered "normal" like we're doing in the menstrual world, could we create more ease for women navigating through that season of life? So if that's you, skip down to the section on using the moon to cycle sync and test it out. When you do, come back and let me know how it went for you. I'd love to start spreading the word to women who need it if my theory really is correct. When I enter into perimenopause in the next decade or so, you bet I'll be testing this theory myself too.

Pregnancy and Postpartum

Congratulations! You're bringing life into the world. As a neonatal therapist myself who works with preemie babies and witnesses the miracle of bringing life into the world each day, I just want to honor the stage of life you're in right now.

During pregnancy, your normal menstrual rhythm stops because your body doesn't need to make a baby. It's already done that. But there's so much change happening inside your body during pregnancy and postpartum. Your hormones can feel all over the place. Your body literally is changing daily as you grow a new little life and then transition after bringing that little one to the world.

All that being said, give yourself a little grace. You're already doing so much! Physically, emotionally, hormonally, and all the ways. This is one season that can be a little challenging to cycle sync because there is so much change, and it's such a season of transition. I have had clients who were cycle syncing and aligning their life well prior to becoming pregnant who continued to notice the same four phases on a monthly rhythm after they became pregnant. This is likely due to the habits and lifestyle patterns they had created.

I had a client of mine who had worked with me for a year prior to becoming pregnant. She was deeply connected to her menstrual rhythm and understanding her body, which as a side, made getting pregnant easier for her. She and I would have weekly one-on-one calls before and after she became pregnant. As her coach and mentor, I could clearly see the same rhythm week to week in her mood, focus, and productivity, even though her hormones were in vastly different states. She'd created a rhythm of balance and a way of living that supported her core needs (more coming in a few chapters on this), and she thrived in this rhythm that she naturally continued to lean into post–becoming pregnant.

But if you're already pregnant or postpartum, I have two recommendations for you.

1. Practice asking yourself how your body feels day to day and learn to attune to your body. This will have payoffs for when you go into labor too. It's going to be a little bit more difficult to predict where you might be and how you might feel a month from now. Yet if you refine the skill of listening to your body in this present moment, you'll be able to meet your needs and feel so much more grounded. It's a great skill if you're desiring to have a natural delivery and need to advocate for yourself during birth. Listening to your body and advocating for yourself is a skill that will support you no matter what season of life you're in.

2. Use the moon to support a continued monthly rhythm, provide a predictable pattern, and create more balance. If you decide to use the moon to create some rhythm, you're definitely going to want to continue option one, and listening to your body will trump the moon for you, but the moon can support you in creating some structure when things feel a little all over the place. (See the upcoming section on using the moon for more details.)

Hormonal Birth Control

There are so many kinds of birth control out there, and all function differently in how they prevent pregnancy. As a generalization, most of them work to prevent ovulation. So that beautiful rise and fall of estrogen and progesterone doesn't happen. When on hormonal birth control, your hormones function predominantly in a flat line throughout the month with a drop in hormones during the time you'd bleed.[14]

As someone who has developed an autoimmune disease likely caused by the use of birth control, I can't hide my prejudice. I've seen hormonal birth control have significant negative impacts on many lives. I've heard stories of women who've come off birth control and realized that they'd been living in sort of a fog for years and hadn't realized it until coming off. Many women report positive mood and personality changes, losing weight, thinking clearer, and more when they remove the artificial hormones within birth control.

It serves a purpose and is necessary for some. I'm not denying the benefits birth control has on preventing pregnancy. Yet birth control has become the answer to many women's health issues. Rather than having adequate interventions and research around conditions such as PCOS or endometriosis, the medical system often defaults to birth control. Personally, I see it as a failure of our system on women and women's health. If you're on birth control for one of these reasons, I'd encourage you to do some research and see if there's an alternative that could support actually healing your

---

[14] Amanda Nottke, "Taming the Cycle: How Does the Pill Work?" Science in the News, 2008, https://sitn.hms.harvard.edu/flash/2008/issue40/.

body rather than masking symptoms. There are many practitioners that are now beginning to support women in creating healing within their bodies rather than focusing predominantly on symptom management. If you're on birth control for any other reason than preventing pregnancy, I encourage you to seek out support from someone who can help you find healing rather than feeling like birth control is your only option.

If you are on birth control for the sake of preventing pregnancy and that's what you feel most comfortable with, I'm so glad you're following what's best for you. If you're needing to prevent pregnancy and would prefer to get off birth control, many women have successfully prevented pregnancy using natural family planning methods and learning to listen to their bodies. There are many tools, such as the Oura Ring and Natural Cycles that make it super simple to know when and when not to use protection or abstain in order to prevent pregnancy.

Regardless, if you're on birth control, the next section on using the moon can help you continue to create that internal rhythm of nature without the experience of the hormonal shifts of your menstrual cycle.

Use the Moon When Your Menstrual Cycle Is Disrupted

In each of these scenarios when your hormones don't follow the normal menstrual cycle rhythm, you can use the moon to help you create a rhythm in your life that feels more balanced and in flow.

The moon operates on a twenty-eight-day cycle just like women do (and did you catch that the sun operates on a twenty-four-hour calendar like men?). Many women already naturally sync up with the rhythm of the moon.[15] When you use the four phases of the moon to sync up your calendar and life, your body feels the same rhythm that you once had when you were cycling or with a regular, predictable cycle. It ensures that you still create the flow and balance in your life that you need.

Initially, you may not feel the energy of each phase. But just as we talked about earlier, your body is smart and learns to adapt to the habits you give it. After a few months of cycling with the moon, your body will be able to start predicting that rhythm and allow you to fully maximize it. Overall, you might not notice the need to sync to the moon if you're on birth control, pregnant, or postmenopausal. But if you're feeling out of balance or like there are parts of your life that aren't getting the attention you want, I challenge you to start leaning into the energy of the moon's rhythms. Living in a cyclical rhythm is by nature the way we were designed.

These four phases can bring intention into each week so you don't feel like you have to focus on and carry everything all the time. While using the hormones of our menstrual cycle can be incredibly powerful, I firmly believe it's this monthly rhythm of creating

---

[15] Sung Ping Law, "The regulation of menstrual cycle and its relationship to the moon," *Acta Obstet Gynecol Scand 65*, no. 1 (January 1986): 45–8, https://doi.org/10.3109/00016348609158228.

balance that has so much power and potential for women, and it's available to you regardless of your menstruation status.

"By following the moon, it's helping me keep balance in my routine even when my little one is going through sleep regression. Normally, I would feel like a dead person but using the moon as a guide with the four cycle phases is helping me listen to my body. I'm so grateful for what I've learned in a short period of time. It's been the direction I needed to get back on my feet with balance and routine."

—Your Cycle Advantage Client

If we look at the laws of nature, there are so many rhythms that exist that support our world in having seasons of rest and productivity. For many of us, we have to unlearn the conditioning of our "success culture" that preaches pushing harder and going harder all year (and month) long.

The moon is a uniquely feminine guide within the laws of nature and is a direct reflection of our feminine menstrual cycle. Regardless of your menstruation status, leaning into the rhythm can support creating the balance you crave without sacrificing your drive or goals.

Here are the four phases of the moon and how they relate to each phase of your cycle:

- New Moon: Your Recharge Phase/Menstrual Phase
- Waxing Moon: Your Accelerate Phase/Follicular Phase

- Full Moon: Your Connect Phase/Ovulatory Phase
- Waning Moon: Your Reflect Phase/Luteal Phase

In the chapters ahead, we'll go through each phase and map out your calendar with what to do in each of these phases to create an easier flow.

The Cycle of Mother Nature

As beings of nature, we operate within cycles just like Mother Nature operates in rhythms, cycles, and seasons. Earth has a season of planning, dormancy, sprouting, and harvesting. The expectation that the earth needs to produce all year long is what's leading to soil depletion and lower nutrient-dense foods. For decades, we've asked earth to continue producing and she's finally telling us she can't do it. She's burnt out.

Women are feeling the same way. Studies have shown more than 33% of working women feel burnt out.[16] But those numbers are for *true burnout*. What about the women who are surviving each day and keep going but suffer under the weight of all they need to get done, working long and late hours, squeezing in work between school drive-through lines, extracurriculars, and relationships?

Regardless if you have a menstrual cycle or not, you were not designed to operate in a go-go-go, Energizer bunny–type fashion. Even if you *want* to. Even if you're like me, highly productive and ambitious. We might think we can do it. And for a

---

[16] Orianna R. Royle, "Women want 'lazy girl jobs' because they're significantly more burned out than men, Gallup finds," Fortune, November 2, 2023, https://fortune.com/2023/11/02/lazy-girl-jobs-burnout-gallup-research/.

while, we can, but without the rhythm of each phase of the cycle, you and I will eventually burn out.

Maybe you lean into your irregular cycle and help support it becoming more rhythmic, or you lean into the moon's rhythm, or maybe you create your own rhythm that allows for time and space for each of the cycle's elements. Whichever you choose, trust that creating a cyclical rhythm in your life will not only make you feel better each day but will allow you to optimize your time, energy, and capacity. Initially, you might not feel like your body or life got the memo, but if you stick with it, trust me . . . you'll be grateful.

Chapter 4:
Recharge Phase: The Power in Your Rest & Reset

What's Happening in the Body: The uterine lining that's built up throughout the month sheds in the form of a period, helping you cleanse and detox.

Core Focus: Resting, recharging, tapping into your intuition, casting your vision, planning out/dreaming your next month

Moon Phase: New Moon

Season of the Year: Winter

Exercise and Nutritional Supports: Low-intensity workouts, such as walking and yoga, combined with nourishing, anti-inflammatory, and iron-rich foods

Business Focus: Create space for your vision, new ideas, intentions, and goal setting. Plan out your calendar and goals.

Your Core Need: Resting and recharging

I went around and around trying to decide which phase of the cycle to start with (because it's literally a cycle, so where does it start?). I often describe our period as the encore to a silent production our cycle is performing all month long. So it seems that it would come as the final phase you and I chat about today. However, there are a few big reasons we're going to talk about it first: your period phase is primary for tapping into your intuition, casting that intuitive vision, and creating a plan of action to execute on it. This phase is also about recharging prior so that you can take major action.

Your Period + Your Intuition

I once read that there are cultures around the world that believe when you're on your period you are the most in tune with your subconscious. It's the time when you're most connected to your own intuition. It's often referred to as the "Wise Woman," the part of you that has a deeper knowing that often defies logic. Being present with yourself and allowing inner self to guide you. Learning to listen to this inner guide may become one of your greatest keys to creating a life you desire. While this inner part of you is available all month long, it is heightened during this phase. She might speak just a bit louder. Maybe your dreams become more vivid and intense. Maybe you start to notice things that feel out of alignment with where you want to go or who you want to become.

Oftentimes I find that women are searching for answers outside of themselves. I'm notorious for always going to someone else for advice or reassurance that the path that I'm on is the correct one. We're searching for the next system, coach, or tool that's going to have the answers to gaining more clients. Yet when we can learn to listen to our own unique voice and inner guidance, we create paths that far surpass even our wildest dreams and desires. We begin to trust the voice within instead of getting caught chasing shiny objects, investing in programs that don't align with our values, and getting stuck trying the latest and greatest new trend.

Learning to listen to your inner voice is the embodiment and transition from "doing" and "going" into "being." Let yourself slow down during this phase not just because you physically need it and it helps you recharge for the next phase but because it allows you to have the space to actually listen. It's hard to allow new ideas and your greatest vision to come into existence when you're so caught up in the busy of the doing. There's so much noise that exists within our world today. There are constant social media posts, notifications, emails, messages, not to mention the endless school notifications, homework slips, and sports snack sign-ups. Without the space to slow down, all this noise blocks out our truest desires and visions. If finding stillness and spaciousness in your life is difficult, like it is for many women who start working with me, start with just this one week of your menstrual phase. Watch what begins to open up for you when you create spaciousness in this week.

The week of your period is a phase for refinement, reorientation, and cleansing. As you physically lose blood and shed the lining of your uterus, imagine yourself shedding away anything else you want to release: limiting beliefs, emotions, people, whatever it is that no longer serves the version of you that you want to become. This creates even more spaciousness and activates the law of vacuum. The law of vacuum is based on the premise that "nature abhors a vacuum."[17] That when there is an empty space, nature

---

[17] "Horror vacui (physics)," Wikipedia, accessed July 4, 2024, https://en.wikipedia.org/wiki/Horror_vacui_(physics).

works to fill that space. This is one of the main principles and tenets within manifestation and the law of attraction. When you release limiting beliefs, things, busy-ness, etc., within your life that are no longer serving you, nature will naturally go to work filling that space. Yet this time you can focus your attention on filling that space with things and thoughts that do serve who and where you're desiring to be and go.

It's one of the biggest reasons I recommend my clients take at least three days off social media and technology during their periods. When you're on technology, there's so much noise coming at you from social media, the media, etc., about what other people are doing and how others are managing their homes and running their businesses that you get distracted from turning inward and figuring out what *you* need to do. These three technology-free days aren't just about getting off social media. It's about bringing the intentionality to disconnect from the opinions of others and tap back into that intuitive part of you. It's about letting you reconnect to that Wise Woman within you. It can be a massive game changer for you and your business.

The Menstrual Phase = Your Visionary Phase

One of the biggest challenges I see when working with entrepreneurs who are endlessly grinding to grow their businesses is that they're often caught in the weeds, running dry on intuitive and inspired actions. There's so much to do that they focus on the actions and moving things forward. This pulls them away from their vision. The visionary space is where the most successful entrepreneurs spend a majority of their time. They spend their time dreaming, creating, and envisioning where they are leading their business while delegating a lot of the *doing* to their team (#goals if you're currently a solopreneur!). It's what allows them to lead their business rather than focus on business tasks. While you and I may not be able to be entirely in that visionary space all the time, routinely coming back to it and reorienting to your vision is totally doable (and necessary!). The period week becomes a reminder to return to your vision and focus on leading your business where you want it to go, ensuring you're still on the path to achieving your goals. But you have to intentionally create the space away from the noise of life to focus on that vision.

When you allow yourself the space to create this vision and reorient to this vision every month, the week of your period can act as your North Star, keeping you on the path to where you want to go and the impact you want to create. As a creative, I'm often pulled into many different ideas. All the ideas I have and all the projects I want to do have likely been the primary reason my business isn't more successful than it is. I *want* to be able to make the fun period-positive stickers, the cycle syncing coloring book, write this book, host the retreats, and all the other things. It's like in the movie *Up* when the dog gets pulled off course when he sees a squirrel. Each new shiny object and idea that comes our way can feel amazing and wonderful. Yet when we have a True North, we can filter those shiny objects and determine which are contributing to the impact we want to create and which are the squirrel distractions keeping us from truly moving forward.

I created a Recharge Phase meditation for you so you can create your next month's vision. You can access it here on the resources page.

https://renaefieck.com/bookbonuses

Activating Your Action Plan

Once you've created the space for the vision, now it's time to create your plan. While I generally recommend spending the first three days resting and creating space for your vision, it's likely you'll start regaining your energy around this time. This is the time of the month I go through my calendar and map everything out. Set your goals and intentions and then look at the nitty-gritty of your calendar to ensure that those goals and intentions have space in your calendar and that you have an actual plan for achieving them.

The mistake I see so many women making when they map out their to-do list is focusing on the big, broad tasks like "work on the podcast" or "clean the house." Yet when we look at each of those tasks, there are a ton of subparts that contribute to getting the task done.

In graduate school, I spent hours and hours creating task analyses. These task analyses literally break down all the parts that go into each task. Many of the simple tasks we do each day, we take for granted all the skill it takes to complete. Something as simple as me sitting here writing this page requires me to have the postural control to hold my body upright, the ability for me to extend my arms and isolate finger movements with graded pressure to hit each key. On top of that, I also need to have the cognition, attention to not just focus on the task but to plan out what I'm going to write. Similarly, a task such as "work on the podcast" has many different types of tasks that go into it. You have to be able to plan the episode, record it, edit it, create graphics for it, write the show notes, publish it, and share it. And each one of those tasks flows best in a different phase of the cycle. So when we look at creating our plan for the month and aligning each of our to-do list items with the phases of our cycle, we need to know all of the subparts of each of those bigger tasks.

Once you've broken down all of your tasks into their subparts, you can prioritize them based on what needs to be done now (urgent) and what can be done later (not urgent). Those that can be done later are the primary tasks you'll align with the different phases of your cycle. Inside my program, Your Cycle Advantage, I show my clients this exact system and how to move through all these tasks. If you want support walking through this, you can learn more about YCA on the resources page.

https://renaefleck.com/bookbonuses

This monthly planning session helps set you up to be proactive throughout the month. And being proactive versus reactive is *everything*. When I start working with a new client who's feeling overwhelmed and burnt out, this is oftentimes one of the areas we can create the biggest change the fastest. When you are stuck in reactive mode instead of proactive mode, it feels like you're constantly putting out fires. While I don't have the scientific data behind it, it feels like it takes twice as much effort to do this because you're constantly feeling a sense of urgency. Not to mention the stress it's putting on your nervous system and keeping you in a sympathetic nervous system state. When you're in that state everything is going to feel urgent. And when your body is in that fight-or-flight response, it shuts down critical thinking. Everything just feels so much harder, takes more time, and feels more stressful.

Even if you create a loose, general plan, you're going to feel way more proactive and balanced than if you're flying by the seat of your pants all month long. Your plans don't have to be incredibly structured in order to be effective.

Your Period Phase Is for Recharging

Physically, when your body is on its period, you generally have lower energy than most other phases of the month. Your body is shedding its uterine lining and losing a lot of blood. For many women, this can leave them feeling pretty drained physically and emotionally. Keep in mind, though, that not everyone feels this way. Some women have described that their luteal phase (more on this later) can leave them feeling lower energy than their periods. I bring this up to 1) let you know if you're feeling that way, it can be normal, and 2) highlight the importance of why you need to listen to your body and start learning your unique rhythms. With your body's energy stores being depleted, it's essential that we focus on recharging.

Think of your body like a Tesla. They can go incredibly fast, but if you don't recharge it, it's not going anywhere. The recharge becomes essential for going fast and maximizing your productivity. Many times, as women, we think we can just keep going without ever recharging. When there is so much to do and get done, we can feel so guilty for taking time off or doing something fun and pleasurable instead of being productive. But does the to-do list ever stop? (*No!*) Where did we embody this belief?

From my experience as someone who has achieved a lot and does a lot, I know that as soon as something gets checked off, there's always five more things to replace it. It seems that the moment when everything is done and we have all this time to relax never comes unless we intentionally create it. Slowing down, relaxing, and resting is not my natural tendency. It's a skill I've had to acquire over the years. If you're feeling the same way, don't worry, you're in good company. Yet learning and practicing this skill of slowing down and recharging is essential for us to operate at our peak.

Recently I heard the story of a marathon coach who asked their athletes to rest for the week prior to a race when the standard is usually just resting the night before. He asked his clients to lean in and trust the process and allow for the extended rest prior to the race to nourish their body and restore their stamina. Then on race day, they ran their personal best races. In the fitness performance space, rest isn't seen as a weakness. It's seen as an essential part of the process and a strategic component to create peak performance. Resting allows athletes to rebuild stronger muscle fibers that have broken down during their workouts. Top athletes are focused not just on building strength and pushing their endurance limits, but they're also focused on maximizing their ability to recover. If it's something that top athletes have learned to incorporate for maximizing their performance, why is it that so many women opt out of the rest and recharging and still expect to perform at their peak?

A year or two ago, we were camping with my dad in an RV park that had gorgeous million-dollar motorhomes. My dad gave my nine-year-old son and nephew slingshots. I watched these two boys giddy as can be, picking up rocks and pulling back the slingshot and watching the rocks fly. The first few times they pulled back, they were a little cautious and only pulled back a little. But as time went on, they got more and more excited and started pulling the rubber band back farther and farther. As they pulled it back farther, the rock began flying farther and farther. To the point I was worried they were going to bust a windshield on one of these RVs and it was going to cost me thousands of dollars to replace.

The thing is, you and I operate like slingshots too. The farther we pull back, the farther we go. Similarly, the more you recharge and recover, the more you can achieve. The menstrual phase is your pull-back of the slingshot. Allow the rest and Recharge Phase of your cycle to fuel you for the rest of the month. And when we talk about the next phase (follicular/Accelerate), it'll make sense that you get your full recharge right before you hit the ground running on your projects and tasks you need to do to execute the vision you create in this phase.

Seriously I geek out on how amazingly this cycle is so intricately designed and makes such logical sense. When we lean into this cycle's beautiful design, it helps us as women feel so much more fulfilled and balanced.

The Slingshot Method has been a game changer for so many women I've worked with. The permission to pull back, rest, recharge, whatever they need to do to achieve their biggest goals eliminates so much guilt nearly instantaneously. It's what allows me and many of my clients to take a week off of the "doing" in our businesses and instead transition into that visionary CEO who can run a thriving business. It's what allows us to redefine productivity and see rest as productive.

If you don't want to sit and do nothing for a week, I'm with you. So instead of thinking about your period week as having to be "time off/resting," what if you thought of it as *recharging*? What things could you do to recharge your tank? Do you enjoy yoga, putting flowers in your kitchen, going for a walk, taking a bubble bath, or breathwork? What things leave you feeling full and replenished? How can you be intentional about infusing your week with more of those things?

I recently received an email from a client who was part of our Cycle Sync Your Biz Workshop.

I've been thinking a lot about our call, and the thing that has been sticking out for me is how we talked about rest. I've been aware of different kinds of rest, beyond just sleeping or being in the tub; there are all kinds of creative rest.

Yet, when we talked about it, I realized that we can even experience this when doing things inside our work!

You made me realize that work can be done as a form of rest if it's something our body is craving as rest.

I was worried about planning the next big push (social media) after finalizing the course (something that I know will take a lot of energy), yet you made me reframe it and pointed out that the way I was looking forward to it and my perspective on it could potentially be where that "push" wouldn't consume energy but could recharge/restore it for me in a creative-rest type of way. That blew my mind, and I loved it.

Rest and recharging are more than kicking back and doing nothing. And it doesn't mean you have to totally check out from your business (unless you want to because there are plenty of months I totally do). It's focusing on what you need to refuel you, and that may look like working in ways that make you excited. Maybe it looks like getting your hands dirty in your garden or working on a craft project. The focus shouldn't be "how do I do nothing" for an entire week. Ask that deeper question of, How do I truly fill my cup in all areas?

It's also not that you don't need to infuse moments of recharging and self-care throughout the month. This week becomes the checkpoint to assess how we've honored ourselves throughout the month and what we need to bring that back into alignment. Caring for ourselves becomes the primary focus during this phase.

During the Recharge Phase, many of my clients give themselves permission to skip the laundry for the week, use paper plates, or eat frozen meals to take the pressure off of "doing it all," knowing that it's not going to all go to shit. They'll get to those things in a week, and prioritizing the recharge for now is going to exponentially help them the rest of the month.

There is no right or wrong to how you recharge, and it may look different month to month and will certainly look different person to person. But what is universal are the three core areas that you need to ensure you're recharging each month: your physical body, your mental/spiritual body, and your emotional body.

Physical Body

Moving your physical body allows you to move energy throughout your lymphatics and nervous system, release tension and resistance, and restore the vehicle that allows you to achieve your goals. Your body physically shows up for you every single day. The past few weeks my right shoulder has been giving me pain because my keyboard and mouse aren't in the most ergonomic position and I've been at my desk working a lot. That pain in my shoulder is impacting not only the way I show up and work, it's taking my attention throughout the entire rest of the day. It's a lingering and nagging pain in the background all the time. The attention it requires is taking space away from my work, being present with my family, and many other areas of my life. When we ignore this pain, it keeps us distracted and limited from showing up in the way we desire. Yet waiting for the pain to show up often means we've waited too long to listen and now our bodies are screaming at us to pay attention.

Our bodies are speaking to us each and every day. Yet many of us have been conditioned not to listen to them. We've been taught to ignore hunger because we're trying to lose weight. We've been taught to push past the fatigue to get a project done. We've been taught to eat all the food on our plates and stuff down our feelings and limit the emotions we show. Honoring and caring for your body impacts how you show up for your life, family, and business.

What ways can you create intention with moving your body, and how do you need to adapt that activity based upon the energy of your cycle's phase (your Recharge Phase may need more yoga and resting while other phases may love high-intensity cardio or weights)?

Where have you been overriding symptoms and signs from your body that it needs your focus and attention?

What ways do you notice your body speaking to you the most?

Mental/Spiritual Body

Your mental/spiritual body focuses on your mindset, cognition, and the energetic state you're in throughout the day. These are the practices that help restore your mind and spirit.

One of the most powerful ways to restore and connect with this spiritual body is to fully connect with the present moment. One of my favorite ways to do this is to close my eyes, take a few deep breaths, and just notice where I am. Try it with me for a second and notice . . . *Is your mind with your body or is it focused on the past or what needs to get done? How can you bring your focus into the current moment and be fully present in the body? What thoughts are filling your head through the day? Are you creating spaciousness in your head to be still without thought, or is your mind constantly racing?*

What practices do you have that help you cultivate more awareness and connection with your mind and spirit, and how can you be intentional with them?

For the past few weeks, I've been focused on getting up earlier in the morning so I can spend some time nurturing this spiritual side of myself. I'll admit that some mornings I spend a full hour in this space, while others it's a quick cup of tea or mushroom coffee before I've got to get the kids out the door.

Yet these moments have had a profound impact on the way I show up throughout the rest of the day. There's something magical about allowing yourself the space to be present with yourself, still with your thoughts, and reconnected with your spirit before anything else happens in the day.

Meditation is just one way to connect with this aspect of yourself. Many of my clients find breathwork, going for a walk, reading your religious texts, gratitude practices, and many more to be incredibly powerful.

When you think of ways you nourish and restore your spiritual and mental body, what comes to mind?

What practices have you already found helpful? Are there any that you think you'd like to try?

Emotional Body

Our emotional bodies encompass all our feelings, emotions, and the way we relate and connect with ourselves and others. Emotional self-care allows us to acknowledge all our emotions and express them in a healthy way rather than bottling them up inside. One of the most powerful ways to expand your awareness around your emotional body and the array of emotions you feel is to be curious about them. Rather than avoiding anger or frustration, honoring the feeling, accepting it, and then getting curious about why you might be feeling that way can allow you to support yourself in a much deeper way.

Breathwork has become a powerful tool for me to lean into both the physical body and the emotional body and allow myself to become present to the emotions I'm feeling. Other tools you can use are journaling, setting boundaries, and engaging in activities that allow you to express your emotions. Recently I've been reading the book *Radical Honesty: How to Transform Your Life By Telling the Truth* by Brad Blanton and have been questioning how often I limit the expression of my emotions based upon the cultural and moral norms of what's considered "right" or "wrong." Based upon his book, very few of us are being truly honest with expressing our emotions, but I'll let you check out his book if it's something you want to dive into further.

There's so much healing that can happen when we allow ourselves to fully express our feelings and emotions. A good cry or a scream has become one of my favorite tools to process stored emotion. Sometimes we don't even know what the emotion is there for or what we're exactly feeling, but the body does. For example, after my last retreat, I drove everyone from Sedona to Phoenix to catch their flights and then afterwards I went back to Sedona. I had another event I was attending later in the week, so I wasn't going home right away. In the car on the way home, I began to cry. I wasn't even sure what all of the emotions I was experiencing were or why my body was crying, but it needed it. I cried nearly the full two hours back to Sedona. I got back to the Airbnb and began cleaning and packing up, continuing to cry. So much transformation happened for my clients during the retreat, and while I was holding space for them to experience those transformations, it didn't lend me space to process any of it. That full-on, good (and long) crying released something after navigating such an intense experience.

What ways do you currently notice that you process emotions?

What ways do you feel like you resist emotions that surface?

Your Core Need for Rest

As much as we'd sometimes like to function as Energizer bunnies, resting and refueling are essential to us as human beings.

Within our nervous system, we have a parasympathetic nervous system (PNS) and sympathetic nervous system (SNS). The SNS is what is most commonly known as the stress response system or the fight-flight response. It modulates your heart rate, blood pressure, and respiration ensuring that you're alert and ready. It also shuts off functions that would be considered non-vital in a life-ordeath situation (digestion, fertility).[18] On the other hand, the parasympathetic system is often referred to as the "rest and digest" system.[19] The balance of these two systems allows our bodies to adapt and respond appropriately to the situations we face.

Both these systems are operating in the background, generally without our awareness. The signs and symptoms of your nervous system's response are often subtle and overlooked. The problem is that overactivation of our SNS has many ramifications, including increased weight gain, heart failure, lower immune system functioning, GI disorders, and so much more.

At this point, chances are we can both agree that building a business isn't always easy. It seems like there's always a longer list of things to do than time to do it. The news, media, and constant emails are all contributing to activating our sympathetic nervous system and putting us in a constant state of fight-or-flight.

Our bodies need the balance of the PNS in order for us to not just survive but thrive. Simply put, our bodies need rest. Without it, the stress can lead to heart attacks, strokes, and many other health problems. Literally, your life depends on you creating space to rest. We need to learn to consciously activate our PNS.[20] It's why we're seeing a trend for things like yoga, meditation, and

---

[18] "Sympathetic Nervous System (SNS): What It Is & Function," Cleveland Clinic, accessed July 4, 2024, https://my.clevelandclinic.org/health/body/23262-sympathetic-nervous-system-sns-fight-or-flight.
[19] "Parasympathetic Nervous System (PSNS): What It Is & Function," Cleveland Clinic, accessed July 4, 2024, https://my.clevelandclinic.org/health/body/23266-parasympathetic-nervous-system-psns.
[20] Brianna Chu, Komal Marwaha, Terrence Sanvictores, Ayoola O. Awosika, and Derek Ayers, *Physiology, Stress Reaction* (Treasure Island, FL: StatPearls Publishing 2024).

breathwork. These modalities allow us to activate the PNS and strengthen our vagus nerve's (one of our primary nerves within the body that runs from our brains down throughout our body and is responsible for many of our PNS responses) response to stress. They aren't tools that we want to utilize only when we're stressed; we want to use them throughout the month (and even more so in the Recharge Phase) so it becomes our body's resting state.

All this to say . . . your body physically needs rest. Your mind needs rest. You need rest. Without it, your body, brain, mental status, and business are going to suffer.

Isn't it beautiful that your body has a monthly reminder to activate this system? Yes, we need to activate it throughout the month too, but there's something about having a week each month when it becomes your core focus.

"My biggest breakthrough is realizing that I can run my business the same way that I manage my health and the rest of my life—by respecting the phases and seasons that I'm in.

I took a two-hour nap yesterday because my body said I needed it and felt fully justified since I'm still in my Recharge Phase. And I didn't allow myself to feel guilty for doing that instead of what I had put on my to-do list for the day."

—*Your Cycle Advantage Client*

If you want to support your body and activate your PNS system, you can find a breathwork session I've recorded for you to help activate an internal state of rest on the book's resource page.

https://renaefleck.com/bookbonuses

Ask yourself, how can I recharge today? How can I support my energy? Where can I let things go and take some rest space?

Recharge Phase Recap

Your Recharge Phase is for . . .

- Recharging, resting, and refueling for the rest of the month
- Creating space for your big visions, setting intentions, and goals
- Releasing and letting go of limiting beliefs, fears, and thoughts that aren't serving that big vision
- Creating new beliefs that support the future version of you that you want to create
- Planning out your month and ensuring your calendar supports your biggest priorities and those things that are going to move the needle in your business

Chapter 5:
Accelerate Phase:
Planning & Creating Your Best Month

What's Happening in the Body: Estrogen and follicle-stimulating hormone and luteinizing hormone are working together to prepare your body for the release of an egg.

Core Focus: Creation, production, exploration, and fulfillment

Moon Phase: Waxing Moon

Season of the Year: Spring

Exercise and Nutritional Supports: High-intensity, HIIT-style workouts with energy-boosting foods rich in fiber, healthy fats, and carbohydrates

Business Focus: Take action on big projects, explore new ideas, create big things in the world.

Your Core Need: Creation and contribution

A few months ago, I gave up coffee. Gasp! I know. I looooovvved coffee. I've spent most of my adult years perfecting my ideal cup of coffee. We even have a fancy Jura espresso machine that brews a perfect blend of espresso with just one button. We tried and tasted hundreds of coffee beans to find the ones we liked. Then one day I stopped.

Since COVID, my body has *not* been the same in many ways. One of those ways is that I noticed an increased strain or stress on my heart each time I'd get sick, even with simple head colds. Then after one head cold, my heart palpitations didn't go away. It was a wild few months of getting super introspective into what was happening to my body. One of the side effects of cycle syncing and getting in tune with your body is that you become a much better advocate for your health because you're so in tune with subtle symptoms. Cutting the coffee and making the switch to mushroom coffee (yes, truly mushrooms), which has next to no caffeine, nearly eliminated the heart symptoms I was having.

Then a week or so ago I decided I was going to drink a regular cup for the heck of it to see what I noticed. Not only did I have weird palpitations again all day, but I was jittery, anxious, and had a hard time staying focused. Before I would have told you that the coffee helped me work better. Grabbing a couple of cups in the morning and a few throughout the day for a natural pick-me-up was the norm and has become so normalized in society. But what if the drag in the afternoon was actually happening *because* of the coffee?

Regardless of if you ditch the coffee and switch to the mushroom coffee (Live Conscious is the brand I'm currently digging), paying attention to how your body focuses and works is key to operating at your peak. Your body already has its own internal pick-me-up systems. It has a rhythm of energy for when you work best, and all we need to do is lean into and trust that rhythm.

The last chapter talked about the Recharge Phase and how that primes you for the slingshot effect. That's because directly after your menstrual phase, your pituitary gland signals for the release of estrogen, which begins to rise and stimulates the development of a follicle inside your ovary. Your uterus lining begins to thicken. Research has shown that your brain literally changes on a "functional, molecular and structural" level throughout your cycle with some research showing increased spatial awareness and critical thinking during the estrogen-dominant phases.[21] This is why your brain is likely to feel the most clear and focused during this phase. This rise in estrogen and the shifts that happen within your brain makes the Accelerate Phase an optimum time for crushing that to-do list and becoming a productivity queen.

As the estrogen begins to climb, you might feel motivated to jump back into projects you haven't really focused on, launch and create new things, start a new workout plan, etc. It's a phase of big momentum, production, and creation. This is the phase of the month that is the most masculine, with much of our energy being focused on producing amazing things. The specific tasks that can go within this phase can vary based on all the things you need to get done in your life and business. Many of my clients and I use this phase to map out new programs, rework funnels, crunch numbers,

---

[21] Julia Sacher, Hadas Okon-Singer, and Arno Villringer, "Evidence from neuroimaging for the role of the menstrual cycle in the interplay of emotion and cognition," *Frontiers in Human Neuroscience* 7, no. 374 (July 2013), https://doi.org/10.3389/fnhum.2013.00374.

create a new webinar, set up ads, etc. Two key questions you can ask yourself are . . .

- What tasks need to be done and will make the biggest movement in my business?
- What tasks need to be done that I continuously put off doing?

Both of these types of tasks can be done during this phase and are more effective to do now.

This used to be my favorite phase, and it often is for highly ambitious women, because we are used to trying to function like we're in this phase all month long. Maybe you're working late into the night because you *need* to get something done and forcing yourself to show up on social media or continue with high-intensity workouts and strength training when all you really want to do is hide behind your computer or go for a walk. I'm sure many ambitious women can relate. While it would be amazing to have this "go" energy all the time, our bodies cannot sustain it that long.

It's no coincidence that you come off your Recharge Phase primed to head straight into your Accelerate Phase. You're fully recharged and restored and ready to crush those biggest or most challenging projects. When you're fully recovered, you actually enter this phase with more energy and momentum than when you push through your recharge.

So ask yourself . . .

- What are the projects I know need my focus and attention?

- What tasks do I keep putting off because they aren't my favorite?
- What tasks require the most critical and logical thinking?

Taking Inspired Action

If you've allowed yourself to adequately recharge and refuel during your period, you're going to be blown away by what you can accomplish in this phase. I call it the Accelerate Phase because it truly feels like an acceleration. It's like a new piece of Play-Doh. Your ideas and visions are the fresh Doh just taken out of the container of your Recharge Phase. Now this Accelerate Phase is your opportunity to mold and sculpt that Doh into a masterpiece. I mean, I'm not sure we can sculpt Play-Doh into a masterpiece, but you get the point. The intuitive hits and inspirations you had are ready for you to start taking *inspired action* on them.

Did you catch that? Inspired actions are actions that come from an internal source. Inspired actions are what you're meant to be doing versus what someone else says you "should" be doing or what you see everyone else doing. Inspired action allows you to innovate and create new ideas and truly become a thought leader in your industry.

When you take inspired action, you feel aligned with your decisions and strategies, no matter how they may differ from the mainstream. When you follow these intuitive nudges, you truly begin to lead instead of being a follower. There are a lot of business strategists and self-proclaimed experts out there telling you to use or not use Facebook groups, buy ads or stay away, do this for maximum productivity instead of that. With so many conflicting ideas floating out there, it's essential for you to decipher and discern what's right for *you* so that you can take deliberate, inspired, aligned actions.

When you're taking inspired action, the high-productivity hustle of this phase doesn't feel like a hustle. It's a good hustle. Like those days when you just spend hours pounding away and it feels *so good!* It doesn't feel exhausting. It feels exhilarating. You feel accomplished. You feel so productive.

You might even feel like you need to sleep less—staying up late and getting up early hustling on your projects. Research has shown that your menstrual cycle does have a direct impact on how you sleep, with women more likely to struggle with quality sleep in their luteal and menstrual phases and needing less sleep during the follicular and ovulatory phases because the quality is so much better.[22] Your body gets the sleep it needs, and then you're on your way again.

As I said, this phase of your month is the most masculine of any of the other phases. However, the difference is that as women, we weren't designed to work in this masculine way all month long. We have a week of this hardcore "doing" and then each of the other phases' focus is different. However, when you've adequately rested and recharged in your menstrual phase and activated the slingshot effect, you'll be able to produce more in this one week than if you push through the whole month.

------

[22] Fiona C. Baker and Kathryn Aldrich Lee, "Menstrual Cycle Effects on Sleep," *Sleep Med Clin 13*, no. 3 (September 2018): 283–294, https://doi.org/10.1016/j.jsmc.2018.04.002.

After two or three years building my first business in the network marketing space, I wasn't seeing the success I was truly after; the goals just kept moving further out. I had checked all the boxes, done everything I was supposed to, and felt like rather than gaining the freedom I desired, I was just working harder. I was working *all the time*. I was sending DMs while on my lunch break, while pumping and eating, all at the same time. When we look at the amount of "doing" I was doing, it was a lot. But I was exhausted and burnt out and questioning whether or not I had what it took to succeed. I reached out to my mentor, and when I shared with her all I was doing, her response was, "Renae, business is a numbers game. If you aren't getting the outcomes you want, you just have to do more." Cue jaw drop. How do you give more when you already feel like there isn't anything left to give? And this is the problem I see happening for so many women when they aren't working with their cycles. Unfortunately, so many women do give up.

Yes, business is about numbers and does require us to know and evaluate our numbers and make strategic moves based on them. But rather than just working harder for bigger numbers, it's about how we increase efficiency to increase numbers. Instead of surrendering to this stifling way of working, how can we align with our body's natural productivity boost so we can do more meaningful work in less time?

Know Your Numbers

One of the misconceptions that women have about creating a feminine-centered business is that it's all about flow and ease and that numbers don't have much to do with it. I often see women making spontaneous moves in their business just because they feel like it, or rather don't feel like doing it. Bringing in the feelings of your body and intuition into your business is sometimes interpreted as operating at the whim of the moment and wherever the wind blows. When operating only from feeling, we run the risk of making decisions from scarcity or other fear-based emotions. Rather, when we're using only numbers, we miss out on the inspired action.

We need both logic and feeling in our business. We need both numbers and intuition. We need both the masculine and the feminine to grow an incredibly strong and sustainable, soul-filling business.

This Accelerate Phase of the cycle leans toward the logic and numbers. It leans toward strategy and making adjustments based on the metrics of your business. It's the masculine energy that lives within your feminine cycle.

We've got to talk about the numbers. Numbers are the data that allow us to see how our business is performing in an objective way. When we see the numbers, we know where to make shifts, changes, and enhancements.

A few years ago, I was in the middle of a launch for Your Cycle Advantage and feeling really frustrated that I wasn't hitting my goals. At the time I was focused predominantly on the revenue I was generating. But revenue is only *one* metric in the entire picture of my business. At the end of that launch, I was significantly below my revenue goal, but my conversion rate was 16%! When the industry norm is between 3% and 5% conversion, my 16% was outperforming significantly. What I originally viewed as an unsuccessful launch because I didn't hit my revenue goals actually became the foundation for repeating it again and again with the focus on expanding my reach and helping more women get exposed to the workshop.

The data transformed the feeling of failure into a wild success. Without evaluating the data, who knows what actions I would have taken by staying in the feeling of failure?

Evaluating your numbers and having systems in place to review them are key to growing your business and a powerful action to take while you're in the Accelerate Phase. While most other admin-based tasks, like budgeting, fall into the Reflect Phase (which we'll cover in Chapter 7), evaluating your numbers is often best in this phase for two reasons.

1. You're less emotional during this phase and can make adjustments and decisions with more logic rather than when your limiting beliefs are strongest. The changes you make during this phase will come out of strategy.
2. You're primed to take quick action on those adjustments and make shifts in your business. (Implementing actions quickly is one of the key habits of highly successful entrepreneurs).

Your follicular/Accelerate Phase is a powerful phase for making massive movements in your business. We benefit from taking inspired action during this phase and tapping into our logical brains to evaluate our numbers.

"Prior to YCA I was feeling scattered and on the hamster wheel in life and business. I was stuck in the hustle of constantly doing things that weren't moving the needle forward. I was putting energy into unnecessary things that were causing me to burn out.

Since joining YCA, I have given myself permission to align with what works for me. I was able to double my revenue, increase my clients, and build a business I love by focusing in on what aligns for me and my body. I've been able to serve both my family and my business in a much bigger way."

—Millie B., Your Cycle Advantage Client

Your Core Need for Creation and Contribution

I struggle with exactly what I want to label this core need, and you might hear me describe it differently if you listen to my podcast or follow me on social media. The follicular/Accelerate Phase is all about production, creation, and contribution. I do believe that each of us is inherently creative and we have a deep desire to create within this world. We're creative by nature.

That creativity may come out through actual art expression and creating masterpieces. It might look like creating thoughts, having powerful conversations, and breaking through current ways of thinking. Maybe you're like me and get so much satisfaction out of cultivating a garden that reaps delicious foods (the peaches I harvest each July through August are *so* worth tending to that tree all year). Or maybe your business is your creative expression.

Whatever it may be, as humans when we feel like we're creating meaningful work, contributing to the world, making a difference, and creating a legacy, we feel more complete. Deep down we crave the feeling that our life has meaning and a purpose. The feeling that what we're doing makes a difference, whether that's on a grand scale of changing society or within our homes or communities, can become such a powerful force in helping us feel balanced.

Accelerate Phase Recap

Your Accelerate Phase is for . . .

- Taking massive, inspired action, whether that be mapping out a webinar or course, planning out a funnel, or revising your current strategies
- Evaluating your numbers and making strategic moves
- Trying and testing new things

Chapter 6:
Connect Phase: Radiate and Magnetize Opportunity and Abundance to You

What's Happening in the Body: Your ovaries have matured a follicle to be released as an egg for fertilization.

Core Focus: Connecting with others and the world

Moon Phase: Full Moon

Season of the Year: Summer

Exercise and Nutritional Supports: Strengthening-based workouts with slow-absorbing carbs and plenty of anti-inflammatory foods; you may notice a craving for more leafy greens and vegetables

Business Focus: Communication, collaboration, presentations, getting your message out into the world

Your Core Need: Connection and relationship to others

Glow, baby, glow! Are you ready to attract and magnetize more clients? If you said yes (I'm guessing you did), this is your phase, so let's get into it.

Say hello to your ovulation phase, or what I like to call your Connect Phase. This phase of the month is so incredibly powerful for creating magnetism for two reasons: your innate glow and feminine attraction energy, and your budding confidence and ability to communicate more clearly.

You're Glowing, Magnetic, and Radiant

We live not far from the San Diego Zoo, and when my kids were little we were at the zoo nearly every week. It was a great way for me to get them out of the house, walk around, and keep my sanity. Many times when we were there, we would see the peacocks flying around the trees throughout the park. They roam the park freely and are often spotted in various trees throughout the zoo.

If you don't know, male peacocks use those beautiful plumes of feathers to attract a mate, just like many animals in the wild kingdom change their bodies to attract a mate. When our new kitten went into heat, it seemed that the entire neighborhood of male cats could tell and started hanging around our house. While you and I don't fluff feathers or howl into the night trying to mate, we change biologically around the time of ovulation. Biologically we're primed to attract a mate so we can reproduce and make a baby. Some research has shown that we actually have physiological changes that impact how beautiful we are or how we smell when ovulating.[23] Other studies have shown that women feel more

---

[23] Žana Stanić, Ajka Pribisalić, Maria Bošković, Jasna Bućan Cvitanić, Kristina Boban, Gabriela Bašković, Antonija Bartulić, Suzana Demo, Ozren Polašek, and Ivana Kolčić, "Does Each Menstrual Cycle Elicit a Distinct Effect on Olfactory and Gustatory Perception?" *Nutrients* 13, no. 8 (August 2021): 2509, https://doi.org/10.3390/nu13082509.

beautiful when ovulating.[24] Our bodies are literally signaling to the world that we're attractive and ready to make a baby.

You might notice your skin just glows a bit more instead of feeling dry or dull. You might feel a little more confident in your clothes. You might notice your libido increasing. Everything just feels a little more on point than any other time of the month. So what would feel great for you to do when you're glowing and feeling more put together? Photoshoots, buying new clothes, getting a haircut, recording social content, and anything else that requires your radiant, beautiful, and confident self.

I'm sure you've had a time when you've stood in the dressing room trying on outfit after outfit and just don't like the way anything fits. Versus other times you go to the store and just love the way everything fits. When you're ovulating, you're going to love the way you look in most of what you try on. I mean, if you're trying to keep your shopping budget down and buy *less* clothes, maybe go shopping when you *aren't* ovulating. Just kidding! (But not really!) Chances are you'll buy far fewer clothes if you shop when you aren't ovulating versus when you are because when you feel like you're glowing, you're going to love the way you look in everything.

The differences are so subtle. Subtle enough that I still have women who don't believe it and they'd rather continue to subscribe to the twenty-four-hour calendar and view our cycles as just an inconvenience. Yet thousands of women are beginning to become

---

[24] S. Craig Roberts, Jan Havlicek, Jaroslav Flegr, Martina Hruskova, Anthony C. Little, Benedict C. Jones, David I. Perrett, and Marion Petrie, "Female facial attractiveness increases during the fertile phase of the menstrual cycle," *Proc Biol Sci. 271*, no. 5 (August 2004): 270–272, https://doi.org/10.1098/rsbl.2004.0174.

aware of these subtle differences and make small tweaks that add up over time.

Confidence and Communication

A few months ago I spoke to a mastermind. I felt in the flow. I felt radiant and confident. New insights, stories, and metaphors just came to me during the training that had the audience awe inspired. I left that training with the feeling of "damn, that was so good!" I didn't stumble over my words. I felt confident. It all just flowed so well. For days after I had women in that group reaching out to me saying how amazing it was and how grateful they were that I'd come to do the training for them.

For many of my clients, they also notice times when they feel this way. They feel like it's easy to show up on social media and connect with their audience. Then just a few weeks later they feel like no matter what they say it comes out wrong and they retake the same video fifty different times before they feel ready to post it. Can you relate?

You might have even noticed this feeling but up till now may not have noticed that it was a cycle or predictable based around your hormones. Now you do!

What else should we do during this confident phase?

Want to ask for a raise at work? This is your time. Want to host a live training and show up in a way that resonates with your clients? Do it during this phase! Want to take action on something big, audacious, and brave? Go for it during this phase!

As a natural introvert who knows networking and collaborating can be vital for the growth of my business, I am so incredibly thankful for this phase. Without it, I probably wouldn't be here writing this book today. I likely would have given up on this whole business gig a long time ago.

If you want to increase your confidence and start taking bolder, more audacious moves in your business, do it in your Connect Phase and be willing to do it scared. Your ovulation/Connect Phase is going to give you an extra dose of confidence and show-upness. Trust me, that confidence will build and grow faster when you're practicing having it than sitting back and waiting for the confidence to one day show up. (P.S. This goes for all areas of your business. If you want to get better with your writing, write more copy. Want more sales? Do more launches or sales calls.) And when we lean into the confidence of this phase, we can get ourselves out there and take bigger and bolder actions than many of the other phases throughout the month.

Body Image and Our Business

Here's my second side note about confidence: Body image issues and body shaming are rampant in our culture. Over the years I've seen many amazing women hesitant to show up and share their message that could literally change lives because they worry about what their body looks like.

In one of our coaching calls inside Your Cycle Advantage, I had a client talk about the struggles she'd had with her body for years related to her weight, infertility, and the other ways she felt her body had failed her. We spent the rest of the call diving in for each woman around the experiences, beliefs, stories, and feelings they had around their bodies. Every woman had a story or experience of trauma, shame, or disconnection with their bodies. These experiences are having a direct impact on how you show up in your business.

Chances are, you aren't going to go live and show up fully and authentically if in the back of your head you're wondering how you look on camera.

Chances are, you aren't going to say yes to that keynote speaking event if you're wondering if you have something you'll feel comfortable wearing.

Healing from years of trauma and insults toward our bodies doesn't happen overnight. It's something I still don't know that I've 100% mastered. (Do we ever?) But I do know that growing to accept and then love yourself for exactly where you are can allow you to open up new opportunities within your life or business.

If you want to start the journey to healing your body and reconnecting with it, I've created a free breathwork session you can access on the book's resource page. Doing this work during your Reflect Phase (more on this in the next chapter) can be incredibly powerful for releasing and creating deeper healing.

Book Bonuses

https://renaefleck.com/bookbonuses

The Power of Using Your Voice On Social Media

If you're like me, trying to keep up with social media while also running your business feels like a full-time job. Even if you hire out and have someone managing your social media, there's much of it that still requires your beautiful face.

I will admit over the course of my business's life, I've spent way too much time and attention on social media just trying to be consistent with posting every day. I look back at some of my earliest posts, and they are literally cringe-worthy. But I'm so grateful that the version of me then believed in the version of me now to keep going. For many years I was hiding behind beautiful photos and thought-out copy. Even the era of dancing and pointing at the screen allowed me to somewhat hide behind the camera. As a hobbyist photographer, being behind the camera is my safe spot.

Then a friend started sharing how much more effective your voice was for connecting with your audience. I started paying attention to my own buying behavior and the coaches I had invested in. Over and over again, it rang true. It wasn't just the people that I connected with through written word, it was the people I saw speak. Something about them made me feel seen and heard when I could see their face and *hear* them speak.

When I wanted to become a Breathwork Facilitator to help my clients deepen their results by deepening their connection with their body through their breath, I had *no* idea where to even go to become a facilitator. I truly mean I had *no* idea. So I posted in a community asking for referrals. I started following all of them on social media. I opted in. I joined email lists. I even had sales calls with a few different companies.

Every time I opened my Instagram account, I would see one particular trainer's face sharing an insight, tool, strategy, or just providing a moment of breathing. I noticed that nearly 80% of her feed is her on camera, using her voice. The other alternate program had a feed filled with videos of breathwork sessions overlaid with music, static images, or quotes. Her energy, her magnetism made me feel connected. Hearing her speak and feel like we aligned is what drew me into her world over any of the others.

Now don't listen to this and think, "Oh, Renae is telling me I have to do only voice videos on social media in order to grow my business," because I truly find value in a variety of media. Allowing your audience to *see* you and *hear* and trust you is a trend that won't go away if you're building your brand.

So if showing up on social media with your face and voice can increase your know-like-trust factor with your audience, how can we increase your ability to show and magnetize them to you?

Your Core Need for Relationship with Others

If you do a quick internet search on the top lessons of the dying, on almost every single one of them there is a lesson regarding valuing the people in your life and choosing relationships over things.

The COVID lockdowns during 2020 gave us evidence to the power isolation has on us as humans with the WHO stating an increase in anxiety and depression by 25% worldwide.[25] We were not created to live in isolation. Conversely, having strong relationships contributes to not only how we feel emotionally but how we feel physically.

Oftentimes when I ask women what one of their biggest motivators for using their cycles is, it often relates to wanting to build their business without having to sacrifice the relationships in their lives. Relationships are such a meaningful part of our existence. This phase is our strongest phase for connecting with other people and deepening those relationships and connections with other people. Whether that's going out for a happy hour or having a date night or playing at the park with the kids, creating intention to foster your relationships during this phase will allow you to not only satisfy your core need for relationships but also help you connect on a much deeper level.

Ovulatory Phase Recap

So, brave one, are you going to get out there and do the big, audacious stuff?

Your Connect Phase is for . . .

- Showing up using your voice and face to create amazing social media content

---

[25] "COVID-19 pandemic triggers 25% increase in prevalence of anxiety and depression worldwide," World Health Organization (WHO), March 2, 2022, https://www.who.int/news/item/02-03-2022-covid-19-triggers-25-increase-in-prevalence-of-anxiety-and-depression-worldwide.

- Performing your launch, live events, trainings, guest speaking, podcasting, speaking on stage, asking for a raise
- Going out on date nights or with friends, networking, and collaborating
- Photoshoots, going shopping for new clothes or makeup, getting haircuts, and anything that requires your beautiful face

Chapter 7:

Reflect Phase: Reflect on Your Growth and Release Whatever Is Holding You Back

What's Happening in the Body: Progesterone begins to rise and support building the uterine lining in preparation for implantation of a fertilized egg.

Core Focus: Inner reflection and self-awareness

Moon Phase: Waning Moon

Season of the Year: Fall

Exercise and Nutritional Supports: Low-intensity workouts, such as walking and yoga, combined with nourishing and B6-rich foods; you may notice an increased craving for carbohydrates

Business Focus: Reflect on what worked and what didn't, progress toward your goals, administrative and organizational tasks, written work

Your Core Need: Connection to yourself

I literally took my shoe off my foot, picked it up, and threw it at my husband who was standing ten feet from me down the hall.

He looked up at me completely dumbfounded. Internally, I felt the same way. I didn't know what had come over me. I just knew that internally I was boiling and angry.

I walked out the front door and went to an open house that was going on around the corner from our house. As I walked around the beautifully staged house, I envisioned having the perfect life in this new home. Dreaming of the life I *wished* I had . . . that was beautiful and perfect. It was the opposite of what I was feeling at that moment: broken and messy. While deep down I knew this was all just staged and an impossible dream, there was a deep shattering inside of me, and I didn't know how to process all the feelings I was experiencing.

Looking back now, I can almost guarantee this moment happened during my luteal phase. I didn't realize it at the time because I knew next to nothing about my hormones. But the deep, heavy, and oftentimes extreme emotions that left me feeling like I couldn't do it anymore were real and deeply intense.

I didn't feel like a raging, angry mom all the time. But when it hit, it hit *HARD!* And it often left me feeling full of regret for getting so angry and overwhelmed by all the emotion.

Fast-forward to that mastermind event when I learned about cycle syncing; I started to realize that these massive mood swings may in fact be related to my cycle. As you move throughout the cycle, right after ovulation, estrogen drops drastically and progesterone kicks in for the remainder of the month. This is a massive switch that happens within our bodies. We *feel* this shift. And some of us feel it intensely.

The intensity of the emotions and the feelings during this phase is why this phase often gets such a negative rap. It's easy to feel triggered, overwhelmed, and emotional. And sometimes . . . for absolutely no good reason other than we're feeling so deeply. It's why it often gets labeled as the PMS phase because it can feel irrational and wild and full of emotions (for you and those around you).

One of the strategies I recommend for women who have irregular periods or who don't have one at all is to notice if they can feel the theme of any of the phases and then impose the next three phases on the calendar. When I was two years postpartum and still didn't have a period but could 1000% feel this phase, this was the phase I started with on my calendar, and then I started mapping out the rest of the month around this phase.

My best friend who had a hysterectomy after her last baby told me that like clockwork every month she could feel these heavy emotions too. Every time I post on social media about the feelings of the luteal phase, it always resonates deeply with my audience. It's a strong phase and often hard to miss. (Which is why it may be one that's easy to spot where you are in your cycle if you don't actually bleed.)

You already know by now that there's a superpower in each of the phases, and this phase is no different. In fact, after I started cycle syncing my life and work, this became my favorite phase of the month. Crazy, right?

In the past, I used to believe that really feeling our emotions was a weakness. I grew up glorifying things like "strength" and "independence." When emotions like sadness, grief, or frustration would bubble up, I'd try to force them back down and not feel them.

Yet over the past few years of my own growth journey, I've begun to recognize the power of truly feeling our emotions and allowing ourselves to process them. Creating the space and safety to actually feel them allows us to reflect on what they're here to teach us, where we need to grow, or somewhere that we need to shift. Our emotional body is what allows us to relate with others and connect with them on a core level. It's a deep part of how we experience empathy.

Our emotions are truly our connection to the world. They are our connection to our bodies and our inner femininity. They are deeply powerful and the main reason this phase becomes so powerful.

Rather than these emotions carrying such a negative connotation, the intensity of this emotional connection allows us to continue growing in many different ways. I could probably write an entire book on the power of connecting with our emotions and our bodies because of the massive transformation that is possible when we reconnect and heal within our bodies. So for the sake of the length of this book, in this chapter, we're going to focus on just three ways we can leverage the power within our luteal phase.

1. Our emotions can be a guiding post for what's truly going on within ourselves and our bodies. Journaling and somatic work are two powerful tools you can use to actually process and reflect

on the emotions you're having throughout the month, release limiting beliefs, and create healing from the inside out.

2. In business, one of the most powerful ways we can connect with our audience and inspire them to take action is through the use of evoking emotion. What better way to connect with your audience, clients, or community than by feeling deep emotions yourself? If you've ever had a time when you wrote an email or social media post and it totally connected with your audience, chances are, you were writing in this phase.

3. The luteal phase and the rise of progesterone can often instigate a "nesting"-type response similar to the end of pregnancy. It can create a deep urge for organization, detail work, and precision. These shifts create a prime time for you to reflect on your goals and intentions for the month. Did the month measure up? Or do you need to make adjustments going into the next month?

Let's dive into these three areas a bit further, shall we?

Using Your Reflect Phase to Release Limiting Beliefs

For so long I thought feeling emotional during my luteal phase was bad and negative. I would try to stuff it down, control it, and then feel guilty when I couldn't and I'd lash out. It's frustrating when each month rolls by and you feel like you want to burn your business down. The intensity of those feelings isn't something many of us have been taught to manage well. And you might be handling it the same way I was, stuffing it down, trying to avoid it, and then feeling guilty for the actions you took in the height of all those emotions. What I've come to learn is that the emotions themselves aren't bad, it's what we do with those emotions that make the biggest difference. It's not the emotion but rather how we respond to it.

While this phase may be heavy on emotions, these feelings aren't something that you need to fix. Feeling emotions is what makes us human. We can't feel positive emotions for their truest intensity without the opposite end of the spectrum. This is what's called the Law of Opposites. It's one of the laws of the universe that allows us to hold the duality and contrast of opposing forces in the world. For example, you can't fully feel the deepness of happiness without the contrast of sadness. Once we learn to accept the emotion and allow ourselves to fully feel it without placing judgment, we find that emotions don't actually control us, they're just part of the experiences of life.

Did you know that the chemical response of an emotion only lasts in the body for ninety seconds?[26] Beyond ninety seconds, we're *choosing* (consciously or unconsciously) to stay with that emotion. Those thoughts, feelings, and beliefs are naturally already coming to the surface. Instead of trying to stuff them down and stay in a state of toxic positivity, when you allow them to surface and accept them, you can then release them.

Imagine for a second two different women. Woman A goes through her luteal phase and gets incredibly moody, irritable, and triggered. She stays with that frustration and it continues to brew.

---

[26] Anna-Marie Watson, "Improve Your Emotional Self-Awareness With This 90-second Rule," Hintsa Performance, September 7, 2022, https://www.hintsa.com/insights/blogs/improve-your-emotional-self-awareness/.

The week may fade, but those emotions didn't actually get processed. The next month, the trauma from the previous month is there now getting triggered again and amplifying the impact. Every month she cycles through, creating years of unprocessed emotions.

Now imagine Woman B. She goes through her luteal phase, still feeling emotional like Woman A. Instead she acknowledges the feeling. She recognizes what made her feel triggered. She accepts the emotion and how it's trying to protect her in some way. She maybe takes a deep breath and pauses to feel it and allow it to be. The ninety seconds of the emotion comes and goes without her staying in the emotional loop of feeling triggered.

Who do you think is going to go through that luteal phase without feeling like a hot fuse ready to burst the entire time?

I will throw in one caveat for my hormone practitioner friends who would shout out that extreme emotions like those I was feeling aren't necessarily normal and may be a sign that your hormones need some support. Personally, I've noticed that over the years of syncing with my cycle and creating a more holistic approach to my body and health, the extremes of each phase have subsided. There's no more angry shoe-throwing over here. Our bodies have some variances, but when our hormones are regulated and balanced, we move through each of the phases smoother. If that's where you are, reach out to me on Instagram @renaefieck, and I'll connect you to some friends who can help you heal and balance your hormones.

For a long time, I had this feeling of "I want to burn my business down" every single month. You get frustrated you aren't hitting your goals or things aren't working the way you want them to. Every month you wonder if it would be easier to give up on your dream and just go back to being an employee. You doubt what you're doing. You doubt the impact you're making on your clients. Doubts and fears surface and spin inside your head and suck you down. It can make you begin to wonder if there's something wrong with you. While just a few weeks earlier you may have been feeling motivated and consistent and excited about your business, this phase kicks in and you can start feeling like a complete failure.

How many times have you felt that way, wondering why it seems so easy for everyone else to show up consistently all the time while for you some weeks just feel so rough? Despite how big your why is, it can leave you sometimes wondering whether or not you have what it takes to be an entrepreneur.

The inner work is a process of understanding the dialogue in our heads, beliefs in our subconscious, and reasons for the actions we take. The mindset work has been responsible for my biggest areas of growth and success. It's also still to this day the area that limits my growth. It's bringing intention to our thoughts and literally rewriting them to support who we want to become. It's the process of expansion and evolution. It's never going to be a destination to which we arrive. Yet what I have found to be the most supportive in creating that inner transformation is three things . . .

I. **Being willing to reflect** on why you do what you do and how you show up rather than just assuming it is the way it is. Our beliefs create our behaviors and our behaviors create our results. So if you haven't been getting the results you want, take a good look at your behaviors and then what beliefs may be creating those behaviors.

2. **Get support.** I was in a coaching container once when someone said, "I just need someone to help pick the spinach out of my teeth." In that, she meant that oftentimes we don't see our own blind spots. Having other coaches illuminate areas of growth has been essential.

3. **Honor the journey.** For a long time, I believed because I wasn't getting the results I wanted, I had some hidden limiting belief that I needed to discover so that I could finally have my breakthrough. Then one day in a breathwork session the facilitator said, "Can we let the limiting beliefs be here? Can we accept them?" and it shattered my world. For so long I'd been doing all the inner work trying to fix the beliefs, yet the reality is we're *always* going to have limiting beliefs. When we excavate one, we're going to have others. The focus on "I have to remove these limiting beliefs *in order for* me to be successful" was the *real belief that was keeping me stuck.*

What would it look like if we honored them for how they serve us and support us rather than feeling like they're the hidden splinter we've got to dig out? When we become present to a limiting belief, we don't have to allow it to continue to guide our actions. But when we focus on the belief that success only happens when we eliminate all our limiting beliefs, we'll constantly feel like we aren't good enough and success will always feel just out of reach.

A practice I've instilled when becoming aware of one of these beliefs is to speak to it as I would a child, my own inner child in fact. I then do two things. One, thank it for how it's showed up for me and kept me safe all this time. Two, acknowledge that while it kept me safe in the past, its job was done and it doesn't need to protect me in the future. The acceptance of where I am today and how these beliefs have supported me and served me in the past has been one of the biggest shifts that has created massive ripples.

"Two big changes have come up for me. One is moving from hopelessness to gratefulness . . . from this feeling that I can never get it right and keep failing. To now, gratitude for my body and its cycles that allow me to really excel in different parts of each month. I am learning to understand and be grateful for the ebbs and flows in my energy.

As a result of that change, I have gained renewed confidence that I can tackle challenges that formerly seemed impossible."

—*Your Cycle Advantage Client*

The reality is your luteal phase becomes the phase that can help open you up to your biggest breakthroughs, transformations, and greatest expansion. It allows your subconscious fears, doubts, and limiting beliefs to come to the surface so you can process them, acknowledge them for how they've served you, and then release them during your period phase to write new empowering beliefs.

The unconscious blocks that are keeping you stuck are more likely to surface in this phase. Remember the period/Recharge

Phase when we talked about how you are most in tune with your subconscious, your vision, what's aligned for you. The luteal phase puts you in an incredible spot to release and create new affirming thoughts that can integrate into your subconscious that help you grow.

Do you see why this phase has become one of my favorite phases?!

I think oftentimes women view their cycles as this never-ending repeating circle until they hit menopause. The truth is when we start to lean into each of the phases (and particularly this phase) we create this upward trajectory.

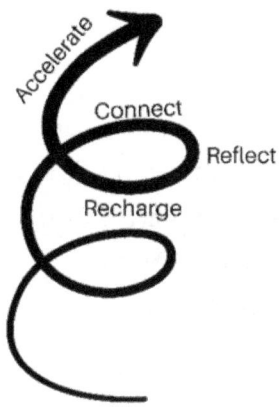

Our growth this month is an expansion on the month prior, and the next month will expand upon this month. Rather than a repeating circle, it becomes an upward spiral of expansion.

That is how we truly embrace the power within our cycles.

Your Luteal Phase for Powerful Writing

So yes, this phase still tends to be your emotional phase, but that emotion can be an incredibly big asset in an industry in which we try to connect with our audiences and get them to take action. How much more powerful is it when your audience says, "Oh my gosh, you're in my head"? Or even more, writing content that your audience was feeling but didn't have the words to even articulate. Take a look at the posts that tend to go viral online. Many of them incur this feeling of "Yes! I feel this way too, and I'm so glad someone said something!" in their readers.

Major brand advertisers know the power of evoking emotion in their advertising because people don't buy based on logic. They buy based on the emotion a specific result or product will give them.

How many times have you done an "ideal audience" exercise where you write out all the things about your ideal client? If you want to create a really good picture of this person, instead of writing things like "this person shops at Target and drives a Honda Odyssey," you write down the things your person is feeling and thinking.

The most effective ideal client exercises are going to help you begin to *understand how you can shift someone's way of thinking or their state of being.* I want to pause on this statement because this can change the way you create in massive ways. Your audience may tell you they just want the how-to content or the value content. But in all reality, they want to feel seen and heard. You want to be the person they trust to provide a solution. When you help shift their way of thinking or being, they will come back to you over and over again.

And that, my friend, is why the Reflect/luteal phase is so incredibly powerful. Because instead of coming up with stuff out of nowhere, you can actually *feel* it yourself. You can empathize with your audience in a way far more connected than at any other time of the month. So rather than feeling heavy and overwhelmed by your emotions, redirect them into becoming an asset for you.

Chances are you've had that moment where you're trying to write and the words just ain't flowing. It feels hard. It feels forced. You might get it done for the sake of meeting a deadline and having it done, but it doesn't feel like your best work. Versus that time you sit down to write and the words just flow and it feels easy. It feels juicy.

I started writing this book for you after I read my friend Courtney St. Croix of Leadher Publishing's book *Authorized: How to Write & Self-Publish a Non-Fiction Book on Amazon.* I wrote nearly 7,500 words in four days because the words and stories just felt like they were flowing. In fact, being in my pajamas sipping my mushroom coffee as I write this is about the only thing I'd want to be doing right now. Add to it that it's a gloomy summer day (thanks, marine layer) and the kids are hanging with some friends. Curling up with my laptop and writing feels *exactly* aligned with my energy right now.

Your Reflect Phase can become a powerhouse for anything you need to write. Even written tasks that don't need the emotional pull will feel easier to write in this phase. Truly, if you're a writer in any fashion within your business, you're going to want to lean into the power of this phase. Whether you're writing legal documents, your next manuscript, or social media content, it will all feel easier to write in your luteal phase.

Let's be honest, you're not going to be able to do every single thing you write in your business in this phase. Life happens, business happens, and not everything in your life is going to sync with your cycle. But when you're in that writer's flow state, lean into it and use it to revise and revamp things you've written previously.

Every time I launch my program, Your Cycle Advantage, or open the doors to the Flow Collective, I go through my sales page, emails, and social posts and revise and update . . . in my Reflect Phase. Every time my message gets clearer and resonates even more. There's so much power in continuing to refine our work rather than always creating from scratch, and this phase is not only a strong emotion phase for the writing, it's actually a very detail-oriented phase as well.

Dot Your I's and Cross Your T's

Normally when I talk about the luteal phase in one of my workshops or at speaking events, I describe it as an "inner phase" of your month and lower energy. But that isn't always true.

In fact, if you've ever had one of those moments when you completely purged your entire closet or kitchen cabinets for no apparent reason or started a new home organization project, it was likely during this phase.

While during my Reflect Phase I'd prefer to not get dressed and stay in PJs or yoga pants all day, that doesn't always equate to "unproductive time." It's about redefining what productivity looks like and allowing ourselves to shift in tasks all month long.

I worked with a coach whose strategies focused on selling every day. During your Accelerate and Connect Phases, selling every day feels good and aligned. But when you get to the Reflect Phase, it doesn't feel good anymore. It feels harder to show up in the DMs and show up on sales calls. But that doesn't mean you're unproductive. It's just that the tasks you're doing have to shift.

During your Reflect Phase, you can focus on the admin tasks in your business. It's a great time to go through your budget and finances, wrap up projects you've started, and get organized. I am notorious for downloading everything to my downloads folder throughout the month and going through and organizing each file and putting it into the appropriate Google Drive folder during my luteal phase. You might use it to empty your email inbox or clean your house.

While a big portion of this book is being written in *one* Reflect Phase (yes, can you believe I've written 10,000 words in less than a week since I decided to start writing?), it's also the phase when I'll spend a lot of time going through it over and over, editing and juicing it up.

All that attention to detail is needed in business too. As more of a visionary, I tend to try to gloss over the details. I'm definitely a "done is better than perfect" type of person. (If you're on my email list and you are a details person, it might make you cringe when you see my typos.) Going through this manuscript and editing has been a lesson in patience and attention to detail for sure. But we thrive when things are organized and complete. When we know where things are, we are more efficient. When we pay attention to the details, we make fewer errors. When our space is decluttered, we allow for more creativity.

When I noticed the shift from feeling all in on sales or big projects to the transition to more admin and detail work, I felt like it was self-sabotage or a distraction from what really needed to be done. I even had coaches and mentors that told me it was. Yet when I realized it was just the phase I was in and leaning into it actually allowed me to dot my I's and cross my T's so that I could effectively rest during the Recharge Phase without feeling like I had a bazillion things on my plate, everything shifted. Essentially the preparation/organization allows you to adequately rest later, and then the rest allows you to be the most productive and operate at your peak, and then the cycle repeats. Perfect design, right?

If your business does tasks more in this admin-type area—for instance, a bookkeeper or admin—this may become your primary productive phase. While for me my Accelerate and Connect Phases are more of my push phase because I'm on camera, speaking, recording social media, etc., your push phase may be in this Reflect Phase. You can be plugging away on your computer in your yoga pants getting tons of work done. This is why assessing your work, tasks, and needs and how they match with your cycle is more than just trying to use a Pinterest graphic or a cycle phase chart.

Taking the four phases exactly as they are and plugging them into standard cycle syncing isn't always going to be best for every woman. We are all unique. Our businesses are unique. Our bodies are unique. And if we truly want to cycle sync our lives and lead from our feminine, it requires us to respond to that uniqueness and design a business and systems that align with our own unique experiences. It requires us to truly listen to our own bodies and our own needs.

Your Core Need for Connection to Yourself

I used to believe that stopping to feel my emotions somehow made me weak. The emphasis was always placed on what I could get done and how I could get through the hard spots. I remember early in my coaching business, I had a client say she didn't want to be in my group because of the toxic positivity. At the time I took great offense to it, yet now, I think she might have been right.

For so long I tried to stay positive and always look at the bright side of things. To this day I still think there's a lesson and everything is happening *for* me, but I've grown to see that the hard feelings, the not-so-good ones, are okay to feel too. Feeling them doesn't lower my vibe. It doesn't make me a negative person. It isn't going to hold me back if I feel sour once in a while. They're part of what makes us human. Embracing sadness allows us to feel joy more deeply. The polarity and the spectrum of emotions are needed.

There's an emphasis in our culture to keep going and push past excuses. Even recently I saw a Mel Robbins reel that basically said don't let your mood dictate your actions. And trust me, I get it! If we let our mood and emotions dictate everything we do, chances are, we wouldn't ever do the hard things or the things that challenge us to grow.

Yet it's a dangerous line to focus on shutting off our connection to ourselves, feelings, and emotions. Shutting off and avoiding the realities of what we're feeling is a huge contributor to why so many women (and men) are facing burnout, exhaustion, and identity crises. They've been stuffing down their true essence and feelings till one day they can't anymore.

What would our society look like if we began to acknowledge our feelings and emotions?

What would it look like if instead of seeing them as weaknesses, we listened to them?

What if we stopped the hustle of life and business and allowed ourselves to truly discover who we are?

Every single month during the luteal phase, you have the opportunity to pause and tune back into yourself. You have a monthly reminder that it's okay to feel. And it's okay to feel all the emotions. And even deeper than that, you can ask yourself the question of "Why am I feeling this way?"

That question can allow you to dig deeper into what's actually going on rather than just trying to brush past it and stay in the high-vibe state. There might be a way you're living that is out of alignment with where you want to be. Or maybe your priorities are all out of whack. These emotions can give you insight into something you need to release and let go of or boundaries you need to set.

The feelings are a signal. The body is constantly sending you signals. **Are you willing to listen to them?**

Reflect Phase Recap

Your Reflect Phase is for . . .

- All types of written content (sales pages, funnels, social media, content)
- Releasing limiting beliefs, doubts, and fears (expansion, baby!)
- Organizational tasks, back admin, "dot your I's, cross your T's" type work
- Finances and bookkeeping

Chapter 8:

Your Seasonal Pulse:
Embracing Each Season of Business

Phew! We've just covered all four of your monthly phases. Pretty mind-blowing, right? After going through these four phases with my clients is when they often give me the "AH! This makes so much sense. This is how I was feeling but just didn't realize there was a rhythm to it or that it was predictable." For many women, that's where they will stop. The awareness of the different phases feels good enough. But you want to go deeper, right? You want to actually lean into the power of your feminine and use your cycle to your advantage, right? Okay, let's keep going!

When I first started learning about the cycle and cycle syncing, I heard people calling the different phases by inner winter, inner spring, inner summer, and inner fall. These names essentially describe what we've just laid out in the previous chapters. It's the rhythm of your month and your menstrual cycle described as seasons. Your menses is your inner winter. Your follicular phase is your inner spring, ovulatory is your summer, and your luteal is your fall.

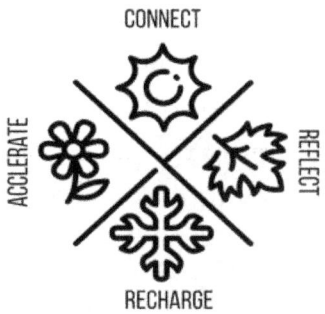

CONNECT

ACCLERATE

REFLECT

RECHARGE

Each of these phases are within your month, but they're also within your year. And when we align our businesses to those seasonal rhythms, we create balance in our businesses that allows for life's seasons to easefully unfold.

Recently I was at a business conference and in a room with many successful entrepreneurs who are running businesses above six figures. One woman raised her hand and vulnerably shared that she feared growing her business more because she feared it would cost her time she wasn't willing to give up . . . time for her family, herself, vacations. She worried that growing more would mean her team would need her more frequently, and she didn't want to give up more freedom. As she shared, many other people in the audience nodded their heads in agreement. Isn't it funny that for so many of us, we get into business with the desire to create freedom, and then as we begin to create it we fear that it will cost us the very thing we desired to create? After the woman in this group shared, the room began a conversation around the importance and the value of creating seasons within our lives and businesses. Internally I was screaming "YESSSS!!" because this is what we need within our businesses. We need to let go of the conditioning around hustle and hard work to achieve our goals. We need to shift the narrative to creating businesses that are built around sustainability and actually help us create the lives we want now and not just when we reach some arbitrary goal in the future. Creating a seasonal rhythm and having a pulse on the energy of each season can enable you to create the growth you desire without it costing you the things you value most.

For Mother's Day one year, my kids bought me a peach tree. It puts out the most delicious peaches, and each year we wait (im)patiently for those delicious peaches. Each winter the tree loses all its leaves. It's the time when I need to prune back any dead branches and help shape the tree so it grows the most efficiently when the leaves return. It tends to be that the more ruthless I am with pruning the tree, the more vibrant it grows come spring. In the spring it buds out with the most beautiful flowers that then turn into budding little peaches. After months of growth, we finally reach fully mature peaches that literally melt in your mouth. As fall comes, the leaves turn vibrant shades of red, orange, and yellow and then fall to the ground. Then the cycle starts itself over again. Each season throughout the year has a purpose.

Imagine if a tree decided one day it was going to skip winter. How well do you think it would produce fruit in the spring if it didn't have the season of dormancy and pruning? In fact, I recently read that most trees *need* that dormancy in order to survive.[27] Without it they die off sooner. Without one of these seasons, my tree wouldn't be able to adequately produce the peaches that are

---

[27] Eileen Campbell, "How Do Trees Survive Winter? The Science of Dormancy," Treehugger, updated February 18, 2022, https://www.treehugger.com/how-do-trees-survive-winter-4864108.

making my mouth water right now just thinking about them. You and your business are the same.

The energy of each season throughout the year matches with the phases of your cycle.

- Winter: Dormancy (planning, goal-setting, resting, recharging)
- Spring: New growth (taking big action)
- Summer: Full blooming (connection, networking, and presence)
- Fall: Harvest (organization, completion, preparing for winter)

Do you see the patterns of the month portrayed in how Mother Nature operates on Earth and with the seasons? You likely notice these rhythms even more if you live in a climate that gets all four of these seasons. Winter makes you feel like you want to cozy up by a fire with some hot chocolate, while summer makes you feel ready to get out on the lake and BBQ with your friends. These rhythms are not only natural but *they are needed.*

Let's Stop Focusing on the Q4 Push

Have you ever heard about the Q4 push, when you push hard at the end of the year to hit those final goals? I was working with a coach who was pushing "a strong quarter four" and going hard to hit big goals at the end of the year. It's a common message we see within the business space. Again, it is intended to be motivational and help encourage people to not give up on their goals. However, if you're like most women I know, quarter four is a busy family season. There are lots of holidays, school functions, holiday parties, etc., so it doesn't have to be a busy season for your business. In fact, for the last two years, I've been intentionally taking off most of December. In December I focus on the bare necessities in my business so my energy and capacity is reserved for my family. But in order to do that, you need to be strategic throughout the rest of the year.

A few years ago, one of my one-on-one coaching clients and I were mapping out her year and when she was planning to launch her programs. She was feeling pressure from another business coach to launch in November or December. As she was sharing with me, I could hear beneath her words that her body was saying she didn't want to. The moment I told her that winter is nature's season of rest and that she didn't have to launch during that season if she didn't want to, I could sense the wave of relaxation that came across her body. Now year after year, she comes back to me and shares how that one a-ha made such a massive shift in the way she runs her business. As we worked together to create her seasonal and cyclical business, letting go of the expectation to push all year and learning to listen to her body within her work allowed her to 2X her business revenue that following year.

You have permission to not push hard for big goals in quarter four (if that's what you want!). You have permission to trade hosting a workshop in December for baking cookies with your family. You have permission to take the summer off with your kids out of school and let your business coast through while you take fun vacations and play at the beach. You literally have permission to build your business the way you want to build it. And it doesn't mean that it will necessarily hurt your revenue. In fact, it may actually be the thing that takes it to the next level.

Having an awareness of the energy of each season and your own season's busyness throughout the year can help you identify your rhythm so you're still hitting your goals. While I wouldn't advise only building your business half of the year, you don't have to work with the same intensity each season of the year. To create a year with a rhythm that allows you to show up for your family and yourself while still moving your business forward, focus on these next steps.

Map Out the Energy of Each Season

If you take a look back at the energy of each season, you see the energy for taking big action on new ideas is spring, right? Spring begins on March 20 or 21 each year. Yet so many women feel pressure to set New Year's resolutions on January 1. Statistics show that most people don't actually follow through with their New Year's resolutions. While part of that could be people attempting to make massive shifts without the proper identity or habits to support those shifts, the other factor is that they're attempting to make big changes in the middle of the winter season. With winter being a season of reflecting, recharging, and planning for our new goals, how much more effective would we be if we actually set First Day of Spring Resolutions instead?

The first step for planning out your year is to actually look at nature's rhythm. Literally, take out a calendar for the year and mark where each season begins so you know what energy that season will naturally have. The first day of each season varies between two days each year so be sure to check the calendar for your year, but here is a rough guide. You can totally go with rough dates for this part too if you want. (Cycling your business and life is a little more "flow" than exactness.)

- First day of winter: December 21
- First day of spring: March 20 (my birthday!)
- First day of summer: June 21
- First day of fall: September 23

Maybe even write across the top of each quarter the theme of each season so as you start filling in and planning the next steps, you have this in the forefront of your mind. If you want the Seasonal Pulse planning guide, check out the book bonuses resource page.

https://renaefleck.com/bookbonuses

Identify Your Core Priorities for Each Season

While ideally we'd align with the seasons of the year with winter being our time of recharging in our business and summer being our peak performance, not all of us are going to have lifestyle rhythms that allow for that (e.g., kids out of school during summer isn't conducive to hitting your business hard). I've had clients whose businesses rely on the holiday season sales and need to push a little harder in that season. Other clients have had spouses deployed, making certain seasons harder for them in business.

You're going to have vacations, weddings, and big life events that need to get scheduled first. You'll also want to put in kids' school breaks so you don't inadvertently schedule a launch right in the middle of spring break. (Been there, done that, wouldn't do it again.)

The combination of the season's energy and your season of life is what allows you to create your Seasonal Pulse. Generally in my business, spring and fall are the months when I push harder in my business. Spring tends to have more guest collaborations, podcasts, and launches. I sort of roll together the energies of the Accelerate Phase and the Connect Phase and make it a hard-hitting phase. Winter and summer tend to be my slow business months because I'm focused more on my family during those phases. Business doesn't have to stop, but the intensity of each season *shifts*.

What do you want to prioritize and schedule first?

What are your core priorities for each season?

What is the energy of each season based on your life's rhythms?

Envision Your Ideal Schedule

So pause for a second and just envision . . . What is that dream vision for your life? In an ideal world, how would you desire to spend your year? Allow yourself to begin crafting that vision now. If you're still working a nine-to-five while you build your side hustle, maybe you can't take off the entire summer now. But how could you begin creating that rhythm in even the smallest of ways? The combination of intention and micro shifts has the power to make massive changes in your life. Inside YCA I have an entire module for my clients to work through deconditioning what society has told them to value and dream and instead lean into crafting a schedule, business, and life that aligns with their dream life. What energy changes do you notice throughout your year? What's your business's rhythm? What's your family's rhythms?

So before you keep reading, pause and start writing it out.

What does your dream schedule look like?

What does your dream year look like?

What days of the week do you want to work?

Some of this dream schedule may not be realistic *right now*, but we're paving the way for that vision to become your reality.

"I've been able to use the awareness of my cycle and phase to plan out each week in a way that feels aligned with where my body is at. Through that, I've actually been able to get things accomplished that I wouldn't have been able to get done as easily.."

-Sara R., Your Cycle Advantage Client

Schedule in Your Revenue-Generating Activities

Not all revenue is the same, and when we think of each quarter, we don't have to do the same tasks each quarter in order to generate revenue. But we *do* need to be generating revenue each quarter in our business. Revenue is the oxygen of our business. It needs to be a priority for our business to grow.

When I started my business, I was so focused on inspiring people that I didn't focus on building revenue. For many years my day job literally paid for me to run my business. I was investing more into my business than I was making and dug myself into a massive business debt hole.

A few years ago, I made a shift to making revenue an actual priority and planning out revenue goals for each quarter (and then within each month). During one of our quarterly planning and goal-setting sessions, one of my clients told me she'd been frustrated with the amount of revenue she'd generated the last quarter. When I had her reflect back on the revenue-generating activities she'd performed that quarter, she realized she hadn't done any! It's hard to generate revenue in our businesses if we aren't doing anything for that. Yet the struggle is that you may not feel the energy or have the space within your life to create a big launch every quarter. That's why it's so important to look at different revenue streams and ways that revenue can flow into your business.

There are two types of revenue we can generate in our business.

1. Active: Your own programs or offers that may require you to launch or fulfill after someone has purchased. This might be a launch, sales calls, workshops, etc.
2. Passive: Revenue that continues to generate without you having to actively create it. Ideas might be an affiliate launch with you doing the launch but it's limited to no fulfillment required of you, payment plans, other more passive affiliate marketing, etc.

Take a look at the calendar you've mapped out and decide which quarter is most aligned to have an active or passive revenue source. How can you use a combination of active and passive income sources throughout the year to hit your goals and stay in alignment with the energy of Seasonal Pulse?

Once you've mapped out your seasons, your priorities, your dream schedule, and your revenue-generating activities, you're ready! It's time to start living in the rhythm of Mother Nature and creating more flow, balance, and abundance.

On the resources page, I have given you my Seasonal Pulse planner sheet to fill in your priorities and revenue-generating activities throughout the year so you can design a year that fits with your lifestyle and your goals.

https://renaefleck.com/bookbonuses

Chapter 9:

The Art of Integrity & Adaptation: Balancing Cycle Syncing When Life Is Unpredictable

There's a pattern I see happen often with women who start using their cycle that leads them to staying stuck in their business. So we're going to call it out now so you don't get stuck in the same pattern. Your cycle can become an incredible asset in your business. It can help you predict when you're going to be at your best. It can help you tap into your intuitive and inspired actions. It can also be used as an excuse.

An excuse for not doing what you've committed to. An excuse for not taking action. An excuse for staying safe and comfortable.

You're probably sitting there thinking, "Oh, Renae, I wouldn't use it that way," but I have seen it so many times. It shows up in statements like:

- "Oh I scheduled my launch for this week, but my energy didn't feel it so I didn't do it."
- "My cycle's been really irregular. I had scheduled this week to write out the next month's content, but when I went to write I couldn't focus."
- "I committed to working out this month, but I woke up today and just can't get motivated. It's probably just the phase I'm in."

Here's the hard truth: Everything isn't going to match 100% of the time. Life happens. Kids get sick. Your cycle varies. Your assistant needs something and you've got to get it to her now.

I can't, in good faith, write a book about aligning your life to your cycle without talking about having integrity with your commitments and how you adapt to where your life and energy takes you.

A few years ago I started adopting the core value of integrity in my business. Once I've committed to something, I'm committed. Which is why I am so careful regarding the things I commit to. Because once I've said yes or given my commitment to something, staying in integrity with that commitment is a high value of mine. Some of my friends joke about how "loose and flowy" I can be while making plans. If we're going to have a dinner party and people are coming over to my house, it's not uncommon for me to give details and plans such as "come over any time after six" versus giving an exact time. I've come to realize that a big part of my "loose and flowy" planning comes from this value to stay in integrity with what I've committed to. It allows for more flexibility and fluidity because once something gets put into my calendar with an exact time, I'm committed to that time and those plans. Holding myself and others to those plans is now a high value of mine. Once I've said 6 p.m., I expect myself and others to be ready at 6 p.m. rather than 6:30 p.m. The commitment and staying true to my word is something that I hold very highly. I've learned that my "loose and flowy" scheduling style is actually a result of me being intentional and cautious about the commitments that I 100% commit to.

Aligning to your cycle allows you to better predict where you're going to have the energy, so it makes it easier to be in integrity with those commitments. If you know next Wednesday is going to land in the middle of your Recharge Phase and someone asks you to do a podcast interview, you can politely decline and ask for an alternate time, or say yes but ensure that you take care of yourself in other ways. Sometimes my clients joke about how it gives you awareness so the Ovulatory You doesn't make plans for the Menstrual You.

The commitment to be in integrity to what you've committed to and aligning with your cycle is a beautiful combination to allow you to set guilt-free boundaries with your time and energy. It allows you to build amazing things in your business while balancing life, your health, and your family.

Have you decided to adopt the core value of integrity into your life and business too? So what do you do when you're sticking with what you committed to, but it doesn't match with your cycle? Because the reality is, life happens. It's bound to happen one of these days that your cycle and your calendar aren't going to match. So what do you do then?

You have two choices:

1. Adapt the task.
2. Adapt your energy.

Adapting the Task

Have you ever heard the analogy of the spoons? Essentially you get spoons of energy and once you run out of spoons, you're either out of spoons or you have to figure out a way to create more spoons. What many women do is have a three-spoon task on their calendar and they attempt to muscle through with only one spoonful of energy. Or they don't do it at all. (But you're gonna operate with integrity and not do that, right?) Rather, when you have a three-spoon task and only one spoon, *you can adapt the task.*

There are ways we can modify or grade the task to align more with where we're feeling energetically and what we have in our reserve tanks to give.

If you need to get food on the table for the family, you have the option to order takeout or throw together some quick quesadillas for the night. If you need to host a coaching call, maybe you decide to lead a grounding meditation rather than an intense coaching session. Think of your social media. What ways could you adapt the way you show up on social media to fit within the energy of your phases and still stay committed to your goal of showing up every day? Maybe you post only B-roll content while you're in your luteal phase, while in your ovulatory phase, you record talking reels. Maybe you repurpose old content when you're in your menstrual phase.

Throughout your business, there are ways that we can grade up or down each task to accommodate our energy without having to just "push through." It's a great exercise in thinking outside the box, creating more solutions, and expanding your possibilities.

Or you can find a way to create two more spoons' worth of energy.

Activating More Energy

Maybe you blast some music and dance around while making dinner to help boost your mood and energy. Maybe you go for a walk or do a workout that allows you to move energy within your body. Maybe you practice a breathwork session that allows you to ground and activate more energy.

Having the awareness of what activates and depletes your energy is a vital skill. What things have you noticed add more energy to your day? What things make you feel that extra little boost when you need it? What are the things that drain your energy (physical, emotional, or spiritual)?

There are going to be times in your life where you have to call upon both of these strategies, and having the resources and tools in your tool belt to be able to adapt is essential.

When I first started coaching women around their cycles, I had quite a few women saying to me, "Renae, I don't even know how to recharge." They would get to the Recharge Phase of their cycle and freeze. The default for them had been to go to social media to recharge, but after I'd shared with them the data around social media actually being an energy drainer, they were left wondering what they could actually do to fill their cups and restore their energy.

Having a resource bank of what I used to call Mind Body Activators (MBAs) or what I now refer to as Rhythm Rechargers (RRs) is essential for allowing yourself to adapt when you need to shift your energy.

As an occupational therapist, it makes sense that when we talk about these MBAs or RRs, we are bringing attention to the body and its connection to the senses and how that shifts and changes your energy. We can use our physical body to help us support our nervous system and create either energy activation or energy grounding. We get to choose what we need and how we use it. How we choose to use our sensory system and nervous system activation can shift and change how we're feeling in a moment and help us gain the energy we need to support where we are in our cycle.

Here's a list of ideas to help get you started.

Energy Activators

- Breathwork using an activating breath pattern
- Dancing and singing wildly around your living room
- Rolling the windows down while you're driving
- A HIIT or weightlifting workout that gets you all sweaty
- Eating a meal with lots of flavors and sensations (Note on this: Carbs or foods that sit in the bottom of your belly may make you feel sluggish after. I'd stick to a rainbow of fruits and veggies and proteins for this one.)

Energy Grounders

- Deep pressure massage or giving yourself a squeeze hug
- A bubble bath with a candle
- Closing your eyes and tuning into your breath or a breathwork session focused on grounding
- Coloring in an adult coloring book (*Cycle Sync With Your Period Coloring Book* is available on Amazon, and I highly recommend it to get double benefits for your body and learning about your cycle.)
- A grounding breathwork session

"Gone are the days when I just want to lock myself away. Gone are the days when I'm just snapping at my family and everyone around me.

I still have lower moods and energy but I don't worry about them because I know when they are coming and how to adjust with them."

-Catherine S., Your Cycle Advantage Client

Adopting Adaptability

Over the years I've had to learn to adopt this idea of adaptability in my life, and I invite you to do the same. Adaptability allows us to enter into our days with structure but allows for the fluidity for things to change. We can create flow within structure.

We can view cycle syncing as this rigid structure in which we have to schedule all of our tasks and stay within those bounds. Yet then, aren't we leaning back into that masculine way of being?

When I say to create your structure with fluidity to allow for things to shift and change, what does that look like for you? What would it look like for you to truly embody the feeling of flow in your life? The knowing that no matter what happens you have the capacity to shift and realign at any given moment. This is the embodiment of your feminine essence. The ability to go with the flow and adapt to life as it comes. The ability to feel into the present moment. This is one of the most truly feminine qualities we can embody. And this is what expands our possibility.

Imagine for a second a river that's weaving through a mountainside. It flows with a steady stream down the mountain. If one of my kids comes along and throws a giant boulder into the river, the river doesn't stop moving. It splits around the river, changes course, and continues on. When there's a bend in the mountain, the river flows around it.

This imagery has been a game changer for me. So often I would hold tight to my expectations, my schedule, and my structure, and when it didn't go according to plan, I'd be white-knuckling it with the internal fire rising inside of me, frustrated that I wasn't getting done what needed to be. It can leave you feeling short-tempered and fiery with your family. It can leave you feeling untethered and ungrounded. But when we switch that imagery to that of the river, we know that there will always be bends. There will always be rocks thrown into the middle of life, but you have the capacity to shift and continue flowing. There's something about "expecting" the unexpected that makes it easier for us to adapt to it. Knowing that life is going to happen, how can we embrace it before it even comes our way? How can we feel so grounded and connected to ourselves that we flow with the obstacles that arise?

As you read this book, there may have been things that felt out of alignment with your body and your business. Not everyone's life or business functions exactly the same. Allow yourself the freedom to adjust and adapt these concepts to create your own rhythm. I have had clients who work predominantly in the admin space as an executive assistant or bookkeeper who noticed that the majority of their heavy workload is them, solo, behind the computer. For them, we structured their month so that their Reflect Phase and even some of the Recharge Phase became their predominant work phase. Then when they felt more energy and didn't want to be sitting behind the computer, they focused on spending time with their family and playing. Other women I've worked with have noticed dips in their energy around the time of ovulation instead of feeling at their height. All of these variances are beautiful and wonderful. It's what makes us unique human beings. It's also what encourages us to embody our own uniqueness and our own rhythms of flow and balance rather than sticking to the rigidity of the phases exactly as I've spelled out.

Don't walk away from this book taking what I've shared and creating another structure that has to be rigidly kept.

Cycle syncing isn't a rigid structure in which you have to exercise, eat, sleep, or work in a particular way. To truly embody your cycle is to embody this essence of flow and adaptability into all areas of your life. **To embody your cycle is to fully love, honor,**

and accept all parts of your story and journey. The embodiment of your femininity and your cycle is about trusting the process and knowing that where you're going is exactly where you need to be, despite all the plans and structure your logical side created for you.

For a long time I spent a majority of my programs teaching my clients the specific steps of using their cycle in their businesses. We'd go through the exact cycle phases and their business and design a system that worked for them. Matching my tasks up with my hormones. But I noticed there was a key difference between those who were using it just like any other system they'd tried before and those who embodied it.

The ones who were able to ride with the transitions of their cycle no matter what it looked like and no matter what life threw at them—they were the ones who transitioned from using cycle syncing as a specific how-to and more as the foundation for embracing their feminine. Cycle syncing their business became the foundation for understanding how to listen to their bodies. They were able to understand the unique language of their bodies. When you listen and turn inward, you open up the space to begin listening to your intuition and inner guidance. You have the power to adjust and flow with whatever life throws at you. It's in allowing yourself to *lead from within.* This is the essence of embracing your true feminine.

Lean into your rhythm. Reconnect with and love your body. Learn to listen to and trust your body.

In a historically male-dominated society, it's easy for us to get swept into living our lives with the same rhythm as men. As women, we don't need to be like men to be powerful. We don't need to be like men to achieve our goals and live our dreams.

We need our feminine rhythms, flow, and balance.

We need our feminine.

Chapter 10:
The Magic of Allowing:
How Spoon-Bending Transformed My
Perspective

I just got back from a retreat where we all participated in a spoon-bending exercise. When I say spoon-bending, I don't mean bending the spoon with brute force and muscle, but by entering a state in your mind where the spoon becomes like putty and easily pliable.

I had recently seen someone else do it on Insta stories and was super excited to do it myself.

We started off by practicing detachment by flipping coins. The goal was to watch what your mind does and where it goes as you release the outcome. The goal was to flip tails. I had zero attachment to what I flipped and ended up flipping twelve straight tails in a row before my mind went to "Holy crap! That's wild. I just hit twelve straight tails" and then immediately I flipped heads. As soon as I let myself get back to "the outcome doesn't matter," it went back to tails again. (It was truly wild!)

So then we entered into meditation for the spoon-bending experience. I felt calm and relaxed and detached. As soon as we were told to pick up the spoon, I could feel my heart begin to race, feeling like it was going to beat out of my chest. I knew this was all happening because I was attached to how excited I was to be going through this experience. But in full honesty, I really wanted to bend the spoon.

I focused on my breath. Focused on slowing down my heart rate and continued to follow as she guided us throughout the meditation until I reached a state of complete emotional and energetic intensity and started to notice my body rocking back and forth. As I rocked back and forth, I could feel my arms moving up and down with the spoon sort of "wobbling" in my hand. I wasn't paying attention to the spoon. I was focused on the emotions I was feeling.

As soon as I heard the words, "Now bend your spoon," my body stopped rocking and the spoon went rigid again. Then I opened my eyes to a completely normal-shaped spoon. Other friends around the room had spun their spoons into elaborate circles and spirals, while mine sat there exactly as it was before we started.

Not going to lie that my first emotion was disappointment, and if I were being completely honest, probably shame. The feeling of "Why didn't I have what it takes" and "Why were others able to but I couldn't" came flooding in. Then I started to realize that regardless of whether the spoon bent or not, it was actually exactly what I needed, and I started asking myself what the straight spoon was trying to teach me.

And then it clicked.

I've grown up with the mantra "hard work equals success" and have noticed how much I force my way to success. Prior to the spoon-bending, I was attached to the belief that if I wanted it bad enough and focused hard enough on it, that it would happen. When in fact, what I was being called to do was to release the outcome and allow it to be.

If you remember way back to the beginning of the book, I challenged you to begin embracing the word *allow* in your life. I am living and breathing that practice. It's not something that comes naturally to me. My natural tendencies are to *do* and to *go* (the masculine energy), but the feminine energies of *be*, *allow*, and *receive* have been beckoning me for more attention.

It's common in our culture, especially in business, to praise the doing and the going. And 100%, taking inspired action is required to see your business grow. But there is strength in leaning into your feminine and allowing yourself to *be* and, instead of *doing*, to *achieve*. There is a beautiful strength in allowing yourself to receive instead.

In order for you and me to shift from this place of focusing on the doing, we have to tap back within ourselves. We have to tap back into our inner feminine. We have to tap back into our emotions and our bodies.

When I was writing this chapter, I was in the middle of a tropical storm in San Diego, and we were advised not to leave the house due to the expected rains and 40-mph winds. So my family decided to watch *Star Wars* because of our recent trip to Disneyland. There was a scene when Luke Skywalker is practicing with his lightsaber and Obi-Wan puts a helmet over his face so that he can't see and tells him to trust his instinct. That is what I invite you to do as you begin on this journey of trusting yourself and your body.

Many women may read this book or see other cycle syncing strategies, but few will embrace the power of truly leaning into the feminine because they are missing out on truly trusting their own instinct and intuition.

Learning to use your cycle to your advantage and embrace your body is just the beginning. Leaning into the feminine goes beyond taking the four phases and imposing them onto your calendar. Leaning into your feminine requires you to fully accept your emotions, your past, your body, and your future. It requires you to become fully aware of and fully accept all parts of you.

A few scenes later in the movie, Obi-Wan says, "There are alternatives to fighting."[28] When we look at scaling our businesses and balancing all the demands of life, there are alternatives to hustling, fighting, and forcing ourselves through. And I hope that this book has begun to pave the way for you to create the business of your dreams without the fight.

Throughout this book, you've learned about the rhythms of your cycle and how they can become a superpower without your business. Your first step is simply to become aware and start to notice. Then as you continue your journey, you can continue to

---

[28] Alec Guinness as Ben Obi-Wan Kenobi in *Star Wars: Episode IV - A New Hope*, directed by George Lucas, 20th Century Studios, 1977.

embody the feminine power within you. This femininity within you is what makes your message magnetic. It's the beautiful confidence that allows you to fully accept yourself and speak truths that change lives.

Just four months after that initial spoon-bending experience, I had the opportunity to do it again. Who I was entering this experience the second time was a completely different person from who I was just four months prior. My "failed" spoon-bending experience was the catalyst for creating so much change within me that ultimately changed how I run my business and serve my clients. It actually led me to feeling like I'd been teaching cycle syncing all wrong. I'd been teaching women how to focus on the masculine aspects of using their cycles—how to put it in their calendars and align their schedules for maximum productivity. What I didn't know was that I was missing the true embodiment of the feminine essence and how when women are truly within their feminine, that's when we create the greatest ease, magnetism, and flow.

These are three stages to embodying your feminine.

Stage 1: Awareness

This is likely where you are right now at the end of this book. You've become aware of how your hormones, your body, and your feminine power are impacting the way you show up each day. Just this awareness alone enables women to begin noticing shifts and experiencing the pressure release. Women who stay within this stage may notice they give themselves permission to adjust here and there based on their cycles, but it's more of an afterthought rather than intentionally planned ahead of time. I often have women on social media in my DMs who say, "I'm just going to start tracking my cycle for a while." While tracking your cycle is essential and creates the awareness of what's happening within your body, *only* tracking your cycle limits your ability to actually leverage it.

Stage 2: Integration

This stage is when women begin integrating their cycles with their calendars. It might look like adding your cycle into your calendar or planning out your seasonal rhythms and scheduling your business promotions with your natural rhythms. It often feels a bit more tactical as you try to learn about your own body and cycle and how to match up your business to-do lists. It can feel a bit like a productivity hack or strategy, just like time blocking or the Pomodoro technique. I often see women struggle within this stage as they begin to learn their bodies and how to adjust when life and business don't always align with their bodies. Or when they aren't sure exactly where to put specific tasks because they're still operating within the constructs of there being a "right way" or "best way" to do it.

I designed Your Cycle Advantage to truly support women in these first two stages. It's designed to not only help you go deeper into understanding your cycle and learn to integrate it into your life but also begin the journey into embodying it and your feminine energy within your life and business.

Stage 3: Embodiment

When you've reached this stage, you may not even track your cycle on your calendar each and every single day, but you *know* what your body needs. You understand the language of your body. Making shifts and adjustments to life feels easy because you're trusting your intuition and listening to your body.

This was the phase I was missing for myself, and for my clients. I was helping women use their cycles, but I was missing this much deeper piece of truly helping women embody their own feminine power. This is the phase that many women who are using cycle syncing only for the sake of increasing their productivity are missing. What I realized was that embracing your cycle is just the first step to embracing your femininity and once we go deeper, it has the power to change our entire realities.

Most women have experienced some level of pain, shame, or trauma around the two chakra centers that are known for our feminine power, the sacral chakra and the heart chakra. Stories of infertility, rape, molestation, endometriosis, painful periods, heartbreak, and more have left many women attempting to self-protect and unknowingly disconnecting themselves from their feminine power sources.

As I began this journey of healing my own feminine, predominantly through breathwork and intentionally reconnecting with my sacral and heart centers, I noticed massive shifts in how I was approaching my life and business. The "hard work equals success" and "it's never good enough" mantras began to loosen their hold. I engaged in more pleasurable experiences (in and out of the bedroom) and reconnected with simple pleasures. I noticed more spaciousness, slowness, and contentment. I don't even know that I have all the words to share with you the shifts that I began to notice.

Yet if I were to try to put it into one single word, it would be . . . wholeness.

The feeling of wholeness from just being rather than the constant need to become.

So I entered that second spoon-bending experience, and when I said I was a different human being, I truly mean it.

As the meditation began, I felt my heart centered and grounded. I felt still and calm. It didn't matter whether I bent my spoon or not, I was complete and accepting of whatever the experience was meant to be.

Within a few minutes of the meditation, with waves of gratitude, love, and goodness waving over my entire body, I could begin to feel energy flowing through my body, and my body began swaying with the flow of energy. As I felt the power of gratitude and contentment and the impact I wanted to create for other women to feel the same, my spoon began to twist and bend, continuing till my spoon spiraled around and around.

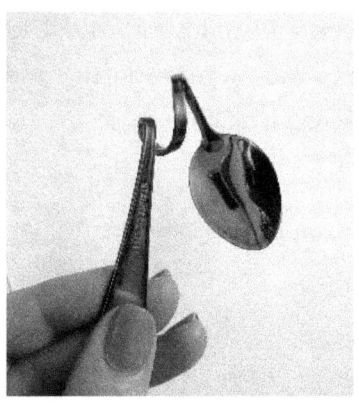

You and I have come a long way through the course of this book. I'm so excited to see what you're able to create and what's going to become possible for you as you begin this journey. You already have everything you need within you to create magic and to do it in the most aligned way.

If you feel ready, go for it!

If you're feeling you want support to go deeper and to truly create that feminine embodiment, I have an exclusive opportunity for you to join our feminine leadership mastermind, the Flow Collective. You can check it out here on the resources page.

https://renaefieck.com/bookbonuses

Either way, if you haven't already, come find me on Instagram @renaefieck and send me a DM letting me know you made it here! I'd love to follow your journey and celebrate with you. Or find me at www.renaefieck.com.

Acknowledgments

I am so overwhelmed with gratitude for everyone who has been part of this journey of seeing this book come to life. First I want to say thank you to my husband, Joe, and kids, Kinsley, Luca, and Britta for not only believing in the dream and vision with me but helping to cultivate and create the space for this dream to actually come to fruition. You all are the reason I pour my heart and soul into everything I do.

I will be forever indebted to my clients who have shared their own journeys and stories with me. Your willingness to trust my guidance and be a part of my community has allowed me the opportunity to further deepen my knowledge and skills. You give me the confidence and the strength to keep going when business feels hard.

Of course, this book likely would have been years out had it not been for my friend, Courtney St. Croix, for lovingly pushing me to write it out now rather than waiting till it was ready. Her book, community, and support made all the pieces of self-publishing this book simple.

About the Author

Renae is a Feminine Leadership and Cycle Syncing coach who has had the honor of empowering hundreds of women to redefine the way they work and build businesses the feminine way.

In 2016, as a new mom to three and a wife to a husband with a brain tumor, she was determined to create a life she loved and jumped with two feet into a side hustle with the hopes of creating financial and time freedom.

In 2019, she was completely burnt out and wondered whether it was in fact possible to raise a family and build a business at the same time.

Fast-forward to 2021 when using her body's natural rhythms allowed her to 5X her revenue, work fewer hours, and feel so much more balanced along the way. All because she discovered the power of her menstrual cycle.

She uses her expertise as an occupational therapist and breathwork facilitator combined with evidence-based neuroscience and spirituality practices to help her clients learn to listen to the language of their bodies and rewire their brains and bodies for a new level of success. She helps high-achieving women unlock the power of their cycles so they can achieve their wildest dreams.

Her method helps women balance the demands of life, make a bigger impact, and get bigger results without adding more stress or needing more time.

Outside of empowering and supporting women, Renae enjoys being outside in nature—from hiking to lounging at the beach to tending to her garden. She and her family have made a home in San Diego, CA, in between traveling and creating memories as they adventure together.

Connect with Renae

Instagram: @renaefieck

YouTube: @renaefieck

Podcast: Cycle Advantage Podcast

TikTok: @renaefieck

Facebook: @risingmoms

Printed in the USA
CPSIA information can be obtained
at www.ICGtesting.com
CBHW070022200924
14691CB00009B/101